that's what what she SAID

women reveal
what men
really need
to know

that's what she said

t. j. jefferson

THREE RIVERS PRESS
NEW YORK

Library of Congress Cataloging-in-Publication Data is
available upon request.

ISBN 978-0-307-45065-4

Printed in the United States of America

Design by Maria Elias

10   9   8   7   6   5   4   3   2   1

First Edition

To my nephew Ishmael Jefferson, who passed away from complications of an asthma attack on January 1, 2008. He was nine years old. I could go on and on about the level of sadness that I feel because he's not here, but I want to keep it positive. He was a great son, a great brother, a great athlete, a great kid. He would have been a great gentleman. Until we meet again,

I love you!

— Uncle T. J.

CONTENTS

FOREWORD

I met T. J. Jefferson in a Los Angeles bar called La Poubelle, which is French for "garbage can." In hindsight it seems only fitting, because we proceeded to spend the next four hours trash-talking each other's favorite football teams. (By the way, I still contend that Walter Payton was a far superior running back to Emmitt Smith.) To give this conversation some context, you must know that I'm a very private person. I don't make fast friends because I have a fear of revealing too much to a complete stranger. However, this is unavoidable with T. J. He has an ability to relate to everyone, from any background, of any age. But his greatest gift is his ability to have a conversation about anything. T. J. is the kind of friend that people become proprietary over because everyone he comes in contact with wants him to be their best friend. And I have had the honor to call him mine.

When T. J. told me he was writing a book about women, I had to take pause. I've known him for almost a decade and I lived with him four of those years. In the time we've been acquainted, I don't ever recall him sustaining an intimate relationship with a woman for more than two weeks. The closest platonic connection with a woman that I ever witnessed him have was with my wife when she and her three daughters moved in to the bachelor pad that T. J. and I were still sharing. Sure, he talked to his mother on the phone and had a handful of girls who were friends, but I certainly wouldn't consider T. J. an expert on the feminine gender. So when he explained to me it was a book that would feature "everything men want to know about women," it made a lot more sense.

There is no one on earth that is more suited to write this book. Socrates said, "A wise man knows what he doesn't know." T. J. has an absolute appreciation and respect for women and a genuine desire to understand them, thus making him an apt pupil. I've met a lot of talkers in my life but very few good listeners. T. J. has the ability to encourage complete strangers to confess things they wouldn't tell their best friend and afterward not feel obligated to give you advice but rather just accept you as you are. And I believe that this gift is what has allowed him to collect these pearls of wisdom.

In closing, I would like to wish my friend the greatest success in this endeavor and I only hope that your journey in the creation of this book will lead you to the relationship I know you desire.

—Ashton Kutcher

that's
what
she
SAID

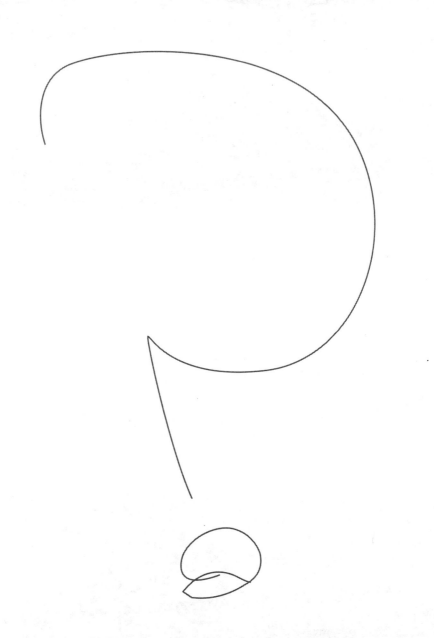

INTRODUCTION: EVERYTHING MEN UNDERSTAND ABOUT WOMEN

It all started off as a joke, really. Back in 2003, I was over at my friend Sarah's house getting ready to go to a movie when she said that she had something for me. Chuckling to herself, she tossed me a book titled *Everything Men Understand About Women*. The back cover gave an extensive breakdown of the contents, and ended with the sentence "After years of extensive research, this book details everything that men understand about women." *Wow*, I thought to myself, *this is going to open some door that will shed light on the most confusing of all creatures—the wily female.* I eagerly opened up the book to find . . . nada. It consisted of nothing but blank pages. Apparently, men don't understand *anything* about the fairer sex. Thanks for nothing. But I took the book anyway.

I gotta admit, women *do* baffle me. I truly can't figure them out, even though I was raised around a lot of women—my mom, sisters, aunts, and cousins. From them I learned the philosophy that you treat a woman the way you'd want your mom or sister to be treated. But sometimes being cool with women can also put a guy someplace he probably didn't set out for—namely, in the "friend zone." If you are there, women think of you as Mr. Nice Guy, which is for all intents and purposes the kiss of death. Now, being the nice guy gets ya daytime hangout sessions, but if she starts to look at you as her buddy, then any chance you might've had to take it further is pretty much done, son! For some reason, as the nice guy you have to work harder to get a girl to see you as date material than you would if you were just some douchebag. I needed this book to help me find answers to the Mr. Nice Guy question, and to many others, too, and I had a suspicion that other men did as well. I had to fill those blank pages.

A few days later I showed the book to some other girlfriends. All of them, after reading the cover and seeing the blank pages, thought it was the funniest thing they'd ever seen. I didn't. Then I struck upon an idea: If men really know nothing about women, I should make it my mission find some stuff out, straight from the horses' mouths. I decided then and there that I'd use those blank pages for the good of men everywhere! And, as an added bonus, I could fill women in on what their fellow ladies were really thinking.

But then I forgot for a while. Three years later, in 2006, as I was getting ready to go to New York for the summer to be the comedy consultant on Wilmer Valderrama's MTV show, *Yo Momma*, I looked at my bookshelf to see if there was anything that I wanted to take with me and saw *Everything Men Understand About Women*. It had just been sitting around for years, waiting to be rediscovered. Remembering what I had originally wanted to do, I figured I'd take the book with me. At worst, it would be a great icebreaker to meet women; at best, I thought maybe I could make something out of this idea. Either way, I decided it wouldn't hurt to try. Turns out it was one of the best moves I ever made.

"In this journey you're the journal, I'm the journalist."
—Rakim

I could have filled the book earlier—and probably easier—if I had just sent out a mass e-mail to a ton of girls and had them each respond with an entry, but the appeal to me was the legwork. Actually going out and meeting different women, talking to them, selling them on this idea, and having them fill up the blank pages on the spot. It made the book feel like a journal, and since women seem to like journals, and they certainly like to talk, the idea made sense. The first few people who wrote in it were friends, and they thought the idea was amazing. I thought that maybe they were just gassing me up because they knew me, but eventually their approval raised my confidence enough that I decided to try it on strangers.

At first, I worked in clubs—which had, sadly, become my natural habitat. It's funny how when women get a few drinks in 'em and start having a good time, they're much more willing to spit some sh*t and lash out at guys. The gas was already there. I just handed over a match. The only problem is that when they're drunk they're sometimes not very clear with their thoughts. Case in point: There was one girl who wrote something during an after-hours party I went to. Two days later we ran into each other and I asked her to sign a release form for the book. "What are you talking about?" she said. "I didn't write in any book." I proceeded to pull the book out and show her what she had written. She looked at it and said, "This isn't my writing . . . Oh, no! This *is* my writing! How drunk *was* I that night?!?" So, as more things like that began to happen, I decided it was time to open up my resource pool. I began to approach women outside of the club scene and expanded my age range a bit. I felt it necessary to concentrate on women over the age of thirty, who would have more life experience and more insight.

I started taking the book with me wherever I went, and when the opportunity to talk to women presented itself, whether it was in a restaurant, taxi, or airplane, I'd reach into my back pocket and produce the book for them. After explaining the title and showing all the blank pages (and after the women's laughter had died down), I'd pose these questions to them: *What do you wish men knew about women? Is there some particular bit of wisdom or knowledge that you wish all men possessed? If you had a little brother or son who was about to enter into the dating world, what advice would you give him so that he wouldn't make the mistakes that most men make?* Well, I guess a lot of women must have had it up to here with men, because most of them jumped at the chance to write down just what was on their minds.

For the most part, I didn't let anyone read anything from the book before they wrote an entry. I didn't want them to be influenced by anything that was already inside. Yes, I was looking for fresh ideas, but also genuine thoughts. And if thirty women wrote "Men should listen," that would mean, obviously, that men better open up their ears if they want to keep their ladies happy. I also went for about a year without reading what was written in the book. I kept a rubber band around it, and as the pages began to fill up, I'd wrap the band around the front cover and the last page that was written on so that I couldn't read any of what was inside. Looking back, I'm not sure why I did that. It's not as if I expected to take the rubber band off and have the book pop open, yell "SURPRISE, MUTH@#*%!!!" and spill its secrets.

> *"I've been in this game for years—it made me an animal.*
> *There's rules to this sh*t, I wrote me a manual."*
> —Notorious B.I.G.

Even after reading every entry in this book, and listening to women as they wrote, I'm not going to claim to be an expert on women; I *still* need help with that myself. Men, don't think of this as a guide to help you pull a girl; think of it as a guide to what you should do once you have her attention. Ladies, I've collected for you some very entertaining examples of what other women are going through. This may make you feel vindicated and have you shouting "Amen, Sister!"—or it might make you glad you aren't that crazy, or that your man isn't such a goof. Take from this book what you will and look at me as the grand facilitator, trying to bring the two sides closer.

The ladies quoted in this book have laid out everything from what types of mistakes men can avoid to what types of things they can successfully do to keep their women around. Because, seriously, isn't that the challenge? Any dude can get lucky once in a while. The challenge is what you do if you want to *keep* her coming around. I'm not saying I agree with all that is written here, but there are definitely jewels to be found in this book—and the rest, well, it's just damn entertaining. I think there is enough information and advice in this book for everyone to find something out about their significant other, as well as gain a little insight into the fairer sex.

As a man, I could only guess about what women wanted us to know. Sometimes you gotta go to the source. If your toilet is backed up, you don't call your dentist, you call a plumber. If you wanna know something about a woman, do what I did—*ask her.* Trust me, she'll be more than happy to let you know what's on her mind.

> *"First of all I wanna thank my connect, the most important*
> *person, with all due respect."*
> —Jay Z

The entries in this book appear as they were written by the contributors. I have tried to organize them by their central messages. I've also peppered my thoughts throughout, commenting on the woman who wrote an entry, an entry itself, or maybe something that was happening as a particular woman wrote her entry. Mind you, I don't claim to speak for every man. I just provide what I think are honest opinions and honest questions about the entries. I like to think that this is a lighthearted look at the ongoing battle of the sexes, and I hope you'll see that my comments are meant more to entertain than to represent the voice of a "male expert." There is no maliciousness intended on my part, and I hope that comes across.

Let me give you an example of one of the entries in the book, one of my favorites. It runs the gamut of topics, touching on many different points. I feel that this entry has something that almost everyone can relate to and learn from, and represents the very best of what I hope this book can offer.

Jennifer aka "The Jenn"

10/04/06

First I would like to start by saying ALL members of the female population want and expect different things. I'd also like to add the fact that there is a SIGNIFICANT difference between what a girl wants and what a woman wants. Girls want you to buy them nice things, to brag about all your materialistic bullshit to their friends (ie. the kind of car you drive, how much $ you make, etc), they want to be the center of your world and demand all your attention with no respect or regard to the fact

that, in order to have a steady and stable relationship each person must have their own ~~XXXX~~ life. Women on the other hand I feel, relate more closely to men.
Please remember this is how I feel and I'm one of millions...

1) we appreciate the small things that take TIME and EFFORT as opposed to MONEY!!!

2) <u>every</u> woman likes to hear you say she's beautiful in the morning, since this is generally when we're @ our worst

3) Be a gentleman <u>MOST</u> of the time, but an asshole every once in a while to keep us in line ... no one wants a pushover or a doormat ... guys do the exalt same w/ us.

4) say what you mean when you mean it, don't hold thing inside until you blow up.

5) If you cheat don't lie ... we <u>ALWAYS</u> know, hello! women's intuition, we can work with the truth <u>NOT</u> with lies ... you dig yourselves a deeper grave remember that.

6) If you're going to cheat don't do it in front of your girl... common sense, but you guys are sometimes retarded!

7) If we're venting to you and you think it's stupid listen anyway and nod with acceptance

8) Give advice when we ASK for it

9) Don't treat us like nuns in a convent we like to get down and freaky too so stop it with the "I can't do you doggie I respect you too much" bullshit

10) Surprising us with the unexpected is always good

11) Find out what stimulates us in bed by asking instead of doing whatyu've always done...every woman likes it differenUty. put the pride aside and ask

12) if we're doing something wrong sexually, explain how you like it

13) never start an argument in front uf other people. keep the drama behind closed doors, and friends and family out of it.

14) If you don't want a dumb bitch don't approach them and ur pick up line be a resumé

15) the biggest thing you have going for you is your ~~ableb~~ ablity to make us laugh. laughter is the key to our soul

ue) If you don't want to be with us anymore be a man and end it insteud of dragging it out... we can handle it!!!.

So I'm sure there's more I can think of, but my hand is tired and I've been sitting on this couch for far too long. I hope this helps and this book idea is GREAT.!!!

What I remember about this is that Jenn literally sat on a couch and wrote for like forty minutes. She clearly put a lot of thought into what she was putting on paper. I remember thinking at the time that if I can inspire someone to get this thoughtful, maybe I'm on to something with this book. I do want to take this opportunity to thank her and all the women who helped make this book possible. Ultimately, my real hope is that these entries will create conversation. With our BlackBerrys, Sidekicks, TiVos, and Xboxes in effect 24/7, good old-fashioned chitchat has practically disappeared. I hope that some of the comments here will get people talking, debating, and thinking about what they've read in these pages—and that goes for both men and women.

getting the
job done!!.

TIME and EFFORT

a big d i

that's enough

FUCK..

CHAPTER 1

SEX

Let's just get this one out of the way. The consensus among all humans is that men cannot live without sex. It controls us; it's all that is on our minds. Honestly, I can't argue with any of that, because it is true. But keep reading, because you're going to find out that even though men are seen as sexually obsessed, women have equally high sexual appetites. They just do a much better job masking their sex drives. That is, until now.

We like it dirty just like you. Men have an angel/mama complex when it gets down to it and they fall hard. They want their girls to be perfectly innocent ... Truth is we can be both—innocent and dirty ... And besides, isn't that more interesting anyway?

Soleil

Soleil is well known for her portrayal of eighties TV icon Punky Brewster and she was the very first woman to take part in my project. She has a point with the innocent-and-dirty thing. Like Ludacris said, "We want a lady in the street, but a freak in the bed." But for some reason, thinking about little Punky in that way just doesn't feel right ...

Always give "muff service" and always listen and try to understand your girl. She may not be perfect all the time, but she means well.

Karla

11-28-06   Page

Size DOES in

fact matter.

Um, okay. Thanks, Page. You've just crushed the hopes of a *lot* of men out there! But you do realize that it goes both ways, right? Ever heard the expression "It was like throwing a hot dog down a hallway"?

Grinding up on a woman's ass when she's dancing ain't the way to get with her! Side note: Women love sex just as much as men do. Or at least that's how I feel!

Kat

What? See, I always thought that dry-humping a girl in the club cut to the chase and let her know what was up . . . and now you're telling me that's not the trick? Sonofa . . .

Many men say they are listening and they really are; however, men need to make sure they communicate and chime in once in a while. Interact with the conversation! Say "yes" and "uh-huh." When a girl wants and communicates she wants sex, you better give! Girls are horny, but guys show it more. All they think about when they see a girl (a hot girl) is sex! However, girls do wanna "do it"! They just don't show it in the same way.

Tiffany

Wait, wait, wait—girls "wanna 'do it'! They just don't show it in the same way"? It would be really helpful, Tiffany, if you told us in which way you do show it. Maybe sitting in front of the TV eating cookie-dough ice cream and watching *Desperate Housewives* is a sign you wanna do it? Helllllllllooo, help a brotha out.

If you push our head while we're giving you a bj, you are a terrible person.

Point taken. And all this time we thought we were just helping out . . . Guess we were wrong.

Annabella

"Just because you lay on top of us ~~does~~ and pump a few times does not mean we will have an orgasm, that only ~~b~~ happens in movies ... and just because we scream does not mean its real," ~~~~

~~always~~

UH-OH!!! For some reason Damone and Stacy in the pool house in *Fast Times at Ridgemont High* come to mind when I read this . . .

Annabella should hope that men embrace her message. With their easy access to a wide world of Internet porn, a lot of young bucks think that jackhammering until the cows come home is the way to please a woman. She makes it crystal clear that this is not the case for her.

Jessica, 24, student
8-17-07

Your love for me should
be stronger than your
PRIDE!!

Also, we were talking about
girls faking it. Personally,
I don't fake it! I want
the guy to know if he's <u>not</u>
getting the job done!!

Personally, I *do* fake it . . . I mean . . .

all girls want to be
treated
Like dirty pirate hookers!

~ bridget
a.ka. Venicehoodrat hooker
8/20/07

AARRGGHH!!! Ye corset-wearin' wench, fetch the good Cap'n his rum an'
two pints of ale, savvy? Something like that, Bridget?

yes, it is true... "No means no!" But many times no means "YES!!" It also means pull my hair, throw me down and make me scream. Learn the diff!

xoxo
dani

Hey, here's something for all girls who agree with this: How about, just for argument's sake and so there's no confusion, you say "yes" when you mean yes? It makes life easier and keeps a little thing that I like to call a "felony" off of my permanent record . . .

Guys don't know much about girls—though they think that they do! . . .

We're a lot hornier than you realize! As much as we like romanticism—that definitely doesn't only turn us on! You're not always the one who wants to get off—we just might take one minute longer. You may have to work a little harder—but damn we're worth it! Snoop's got it right!

Coop

Coop is referencing Snoop Dogg's song "Sexual Eruption." Check out the first verse and you'll know what she is talking about.

Not all women enjoy men that are all over them. We like the challenge as much as you do!

22 yrs old
General Manager

LIL TT

Let me dispel this myth—the majority of men *do not want a challenge*. PERIOD. Yeah, it sounds good to say it, but believe you me, it's not what we want. If we go to the park to play ball, and the team running the court has won four games in a row, yeah, that's a challenge we'll accept. But having to take you out three times just to get a peck on the cheek? We'll usually pass.

- All men fall second to the Jack Rabbit!

- "That Girl" is NOT worth cheating on me with!

- Even though I can be a little CRAZY at times, it's okay, it tends to translate well in the bedroom!

- It's okay to be dirty in the bedroom. I like it, so don't be afraid!

- All men should be handy.

- Girls like porn too!

- There's a 90 percent chance I'll break your heart.

- I don't date bad boys—I FUCK Gangsters!

Cry$tal

The day the Jack Rabbit takes out the trash, kills spiders, mows the lawn, listens to you nag, *and* runs without batteries is the day we men will worry about it. Ummm, the Jack Rabbit doesn't take out the trash . . . does it?

Let's see . . . I could go on for days but I am going to stick to the basics. First of all, we think about and want sex as much as you guys. The only difference is we have a tendency to not always act on it. So all you need to do is find out what puts us over the edge and use it. We will the majority of the time give in. The second bit of info is—a compliment goes pretty far as long as it is unique. The whole, "You look great/pretty" bullshit doesn't work. If you find something that makes a woman an individual then you have nailed it. And last but not least, women like to be taken care of. Yes, a special gift is always a plus, but the smaller things can do so much more. We want to feel protected but not over-protected. It is a man's duty to figure out how to look after his woman. I know these are only the basics and for the most part pretty obvious, but some women try to claim that these don't apply to them. Well, that's bullshit. Oh yeah—one more piece of advice—make sure that in bed it's not a "you give, I give" type of situation. Make it so that it happens when the giver WANTS to give and doesn't feel obligated. So there you go, that's my advice.

Paige

A few women wrote something to the effect of "women think of sex as much as men do." First of all, no you don't. Trust me—I once spent twenty-two hours of a day thinking of Halle Berry in various stages of undress and the other two watching WWE's *Friday Night SmackDown*. That's weird, I know. Whatever.

- Knowing how to ask a woman what she wants sexually is the key. Keeps things fresh and sexy.

- A man who knew how to make a great sauce from scratch would have me locked down for life.

- Keep good beer in the fridge for us. We love spirits too...

Tiffany

ego

flowers + diamonds

Gettin' any.

AMOR...

his lady

CHAPTER 2

LOVE

The word *love* is harder for most men to say than *supercalifragilisticexpialidocious*. It doesn't mean that we don't lo . . . looo . . . loove . . . you; it's just that we're not programmed to say it about anything other than our favorite sports team or food. Women have to understand this and know it in advance when they start a relationship. You know the saying "I can show ya better than I can tell ya"? Check for how your guy shows his love instead of browbeating him for not saying it. And besides, aren't those guys who say they love you on the second date kind of creepy?

Men need to understand we are their woman and not their mama. We need to feel loved and appreciated. A man can get away with a lot and have a lot of freedom IF he takes care of home. THAT'S REAL TALK. Just love us and show us.

Brandi

I think that men forget that women need to be nurtured. Being nurtured does not mean "having sex"—it goes deeper than that. Some men are born with the nurturing quality, some don't have a nurturing bone in their body. Women need it, crave it, especially the ones that didn't grow up with a daddy. Are we looking for the father figure? Maybe . . . Nurturing someone is not material—it's the soft kisses, the touch, that hug that makes you feel safe, like nothing in the world can hurt you. It's that rare but pure form of love.

Heidi Marie

Men need to understand that women want MEN. We want to feel like women. We want you to be strong, protective, and domineering. We want you to be in the driver's seat. We want to feel beautiful and demure. We want you to rise to the occasion. We want to be chased and conquered. We want to be a helpmate to you. A smart man should want a smart woman to assist him on his way to the top. Listen to us and let us know you appreciate us. When a man is truly being a man, we will be your lady, your friend, your backbone, the Robin to your Batman.

T. Lainer

Women love romance, bottom line. We want to be swept off our feet! Flowers, jewelry, random dates ... whatever. If that dies, all is lost. Boys, get it through your heads!!!

Lucy

Don't ever assume a woman knows less than you do. And, most women between twenty-two and thirty-two are desperate for "true love."

Autumn

No matter what they say, every woman wants to be treated like a princess!!! In other words, the same way that their father treated them their entire life (a "good" father).

Chloe

We need the return of the alpha males. Be able to solve anything. Taking care of things can mean an ass-beating or just giving driving directions. Take care of the ladies and they will take care of you!

Jennifer

If Dr. Oz, Rampage Jackson, and Ty Pennington were all able to somehow conceive a baby and that baby were male, he would have a shot with Jennifer when he grew up!

Ask if I want to use your toothbrush.

Piper

I think what she meant by this is if you have a girl staying over (especially if you've been intimate) you should make her feel as comfortable as possible. Using someone else's toothbrush is a bit much, in my opinion, but hey, if that's your thing . . .

Men need to know that even the smartest, most intelligent woman needs to be spooned. The human touch is the most basic of all needs. When she's angry, sad, pugnacious, is when she needs spooning the most. She wants to be kissed on her back, neck, and back of her neck. This does nothing sexually for you, but does wonders for her. Be gentle, be kind, and most of all, eat pussy. It's required after you spoon.

Dawn

My friend Jamie is always complaining that guys spoon only so they can try to get a little. "Spooning leads to forking," she contends. I keep trying to tell her no, that's not true. Every now and then guys like to just curl up with a girl, feel close to her, and have that be it. Thanks a lot, Dawn, for messing that up for me!

Always compliment!

Andrea

GABY (06/25/07)

MUCHO MUCHO AMOR...

MUCHA MUCHA PASION...

Y SOBRETODO IMAGINACON.

Y AÚN MAS IMPORTANTE ES

SER DIFERENTE"

TRANSLATION:

A lot A lot of Love...A lot A lot of Passion...And more than anything IMAGINATION... The most important thing is to be different.

It was important for me to have women from different countries and cultures take part in this project. The entries from foreign women show that no matter where you are from or what your native tongue is, the struggles of men and women to understand and relate to one another are universal.

Life is round like the earth. You get what you give. Always be a giver!

Christine

Act as if . . .

1. You don't know anything about her—but are willing to listen and learn.

2. You are absolutely interested even if you are not!

3. If she has failed, accept the times she has succeeded.

4. She is the ripest strawberry in the whole patch and you want to do nothing but eat her!

5. It is impossible for the two of you to fail. The relation of men and women is always a work in progress!!

Gina Rea and Elisha

You can follow to the letter every bit of advice in this book, walk on your toes for the rest of your life, come home early every night, give me the keys to your car, call me beautiful all the time, become the best lover in the world, a faithful husband, a devoted father, behave 24/7 like a lap dog and if I still complain... don't take it personally. It's God's fault, not mine!

I'm just a woman... or the closest thing to a bottomless barrel.

Shakira

Shakira, Shakira. Her hips do not lie. I went to dinner in New York one night with Ashton, Demi Moore, and a small group of people that included Shakira. After dinner we all headed over to a club called Butter. (That was a hell of a night, let me tell you. Janet was also there. Sadly I didn't meet her, so I wasn't able to get Miss Jackson's assessment of the male/female dynamic. Maybe in the next one.) Anyway... back to Shakira. At first she said she couldn't think of anything really good to write, but she promised that she would e-mail me something later. I figured she's a busy person, so of course I'd never hear from her again. But lo and behold, about two weeks later she e-mailed me this and it turned out to be one of my favorites. That's right, my dudes. Shakira e-mailed ME! Don't hate!

One thing I will say is that no matter how strong, hesitant, or even angry a woman is—when she is feeling down emotionally, physically, mentally—there can never be enough love (you CAN'T cater too much). It will do two things:

1.   Make her realize how amazing you are.

2.   Make her see how wrong or bad she was.

P.S. Women love a guy with good hygiene—take care of yourself—please smell good!!

P.P.S. Trust! You'll get a good response.

P.P.P.S. As I was reading this out loud with men around . . . one other good note: Let a woman finish her sentence and what she's saying. Thank you in advance.

Vanessa Minillo

The most important thing a man can do is appreciate what he has with his lady... and just appreciate her! So many men don't realize how lucky they are when they find a great woman. A good woman is truly hard to find, so when a man finds one he needs to cherish her & not fuck things up! A man should treat a woman the way he'd want his mother or sister treated.

Give her love, respect & lots of great sex! Poetry, flowers & diamonds are good too!

Kendra Cole 30 yrs.
Skybar General Manager
10/6/07

Love, respect, whoopee, poetry, and flowers—all things we can give women for free. Now, diamonds? They're forever—and the relationship had better be, too, before most of us make a trip to De Beers.

Mary Rockwood-Crabtree
Age 35 Makeup Artist, Vegas
married 12 years

Having your mate for a long long time required a true friendship. It all boils down to getting along and willing to put up with each other. If you can't tolerate *everything* about one another it affects everything. Your romantic relationship especially. Basicly if your not nice You aint gettin' any!

I'm surprised that this point wasn't made by more women. I think that you have to *like* the person you're with as much as, if not more than, you *love* them. *Love* can blind you to certain things, but if you truly *like* the person and most things about them, I'd say your ship will sail a bit smoother . . .

Its all about balance.
its about Love, the fairytale
as much as its about
truth and honesty. Its
about losing your self
in the wonder of Love
the beauty the sexiness
the passion... As well
as taking on the
challenges of being
human, the imperfections
A woman wants to
embrace all of it...
If you find a woman
that you can have
this with dont Run from
her. She could be
Just the woman that
will make you a ➝

Better Man. Thats
what we are all
here for in the first
place. To make
one another better
people. Dont be
afraid... Live life
to the fullest...

Cameron

I met Cameron Diaz while she was in the last week of filming the movie *What Happens in Vegas* with Ashton. He had told her about the book before we met, so I had a nice in with her. Even though she agreed to write something when we first met, I didn't want to bother her by constantly asking, so I figured I'd let it come up organically and if it happened, it happened. Well, the last day of filming came around and my window of opportunity was closing. She must have had the book on her mind because as she walked past me outside of a ballroom in Planet Hollywood, where they were taking the pictures for the movie poster, she told me, "I need to write in your book today!" That made me feel great because, honestly, like I said, I didn't want to bother her. But I *really* wanted her in the book. So the day was coming to an end and she and Ashton had only two shots left and the clock was ticking. I sat in on an ADR session in an empty room with just the two of them, the director, the script supervisor, and the sound guy. (ADR, for those who don't know, is basically repeating dialogue so it can be re-recorded clean and free of any background noise.) They finished the session, and as she walked out the door, she turned to me and asked for the book. Holla at ya boy!

Men should know that we are sensitive, shy, emotionally caring, loving and are afraid of letting go. Men want things to fast. We want Romance, Honesty, Truth and a great Sense of humor. We have to put on a attitude just to make sure we don't get hurt.

Be gentle with us. Treat us
with Respect and ~~Use~~ God
looks at us. A beautiful
Jewel

Sheila Escovedo
2/7/08   50 years old
on the plane - to Burbank

I met Ms. Escovedo, better known as Sheila E, when we sat in the same row on a flight. She is of course well known for her hit songs "The Glamorous Life" and "A Love Bizarre," and—with apologies to ?uestlove, Tommy Lee, and Charlie Watts—is the sexiest drummer to ever hit a high hat. Of course I had a little crush on her back in the day, so it was tight being able to meet her and have her take part.

I believe men need to understand that women's emotions are always changing. Being more flexible in their thinking with a woman would help them come to a mutual understanding much quicker. I think men want too much of a black-and-white world, where as women just are not able to be categorized as such. Thank you for letting me be a part of your project. I find it very interesting and refreshing.

Rhoda

> You're very welcome, Rhoda. I hope everyone else will agree with you!

The most important thing is not to take your relationship for granted. I love affection. We're not on a basketball team. I don't want a high five in the morning. I want a hug—a kiss, [some] expression of adoration. A Stone Roses song is coming to my head—"I Wanna Be Adored." That's it. Love is about expression and the human touch feels awesome and keeps love alive. It brings the sparkles to our eyes.

Dani P.

It's simple—women like to be appreciated and loved well. A woman knows when neither is happening. And she rewards him when it is.

Melody

Rewards him? What, like you reward Fido with a treat after he jumps through a hoop for ya? What are we, dogs? Wait a minute . . . Never mind . . .

Become the friend of a female and love her from within, not just for what she looks like outside. Beauty has to be within as well as the physical appearance.

Monique

Always, always have a laugh (every day). We need you. Reassure us when it is not expected. Sweet compliments are better than anything material we could ever get. Kissing is amazing. Be adventurous and risky and unexpected with sex. Telling someone you love them is a gift and blessing and should not be a shield from fear. Practice love with your heart on your sleeve.

Sole

DON'T

- Please know how to spell if you're gonna be an avid texter.

- Don't wear a thong to bed.

- Don't kiss in between my fingers ... on the first date—ever ...

- My boobs aren't here to play with when you're bored.

DO

- Love me. :)

Beth

Beth, we as men greatly disagree; if your boobs aren't there for us to play with, then why would God have made them round like basketballs?

- Men must make women laugh all the time!

- You (men) should understand that women are special. They should be treated like gifts.

- Women will be loyal to their men, so men should be loyal to women.

- You (men) should just love us with all your heart!

Jacin

* Women love to be loved. They cherish your protection and ~~mmm~~ always need to feel safe.

* Our ego isn't nearly as big as yours. We ~~~~ come with an innate confidence that doesn't need ~~approx~~ approval.

* To all single males: We love to feel safe!! We appreciate when you respect our bodies. and love when you ~~me~~ cherish our friends as much as we do.

♡ Jennifer Holt
23 yrs. old
2·16·08

Famed twentieth-century poets the Spice Girls once said, "If you wanna be my lover you gotta get with my friends." I think Jen and the Spices are on the same page!

properly introduce her

from

dog

demp your ass in 2 seconds.

CHAPTER 3

COMMUNICATION

Good communication is essential in almost every aspect of life where two entities are trying to reach a mutually positive outcome. Whether you are bartering with a salesperson for a lower price or trying to resolve a bump in your relationship, communication is key. Let your partner know what's on your mind and how you feel. You'll rarely go wrong. Trust me, most women feel this way; the topic of communication came up a lot in the comments women made in my little book.

Lauren - actress

7/11/07

Call.

We like to be contacted.
(unless you're stalking us,
of course).
But if we're into you,
and you're into us, then
SHOW IT! Mystery is
great, but so is
communication.

Women also fear commitment and, believe it or not, many of us have a hard time expressing our feelings . . . so don't give up on us!

Lacee

Some women do have a hard time expressing their feelings . . . Then one night they get really drunk, show up at your house at 2:30 in the morning, and decide to have a fashion show while going through your closet. Now *that's* the type of expression I can get with . . . Not that it's ever happened to me ☺ . . .

Persistence is EVERYTHING.

Anna

Note: Sometimes being overly persistent leads to something the authorities refer to as a "restraining order."

Confidence is everything!! Well, so is humor. Cooking skills help also. Men need to understand that girls overanalyze everything. So, please try to explain your feelings in detail so there is no room for confusion. Thanks, boys!!

Alexis

Confidence, humor, and cooking skills? Alexis is looking to meet Anthony Bourdain.

ALISON WAITE
PLAYBOYS MISS MAY 2006
♡ Listening is key —
If you listen to us
you will find all the
answers ... what we
like (and eyes of do mean
in bed as well ☺)

So I'm on a flight from LAX to Vegas and, how YOU doin', I'm sitting next to
Alison. Ya gotta love it when a Playmate sits next to you on a flight—sure as
hell beats sitting next to a hairy guy with sardine breath . . .

Guys should always have an open and honest relationship. Some men should learn how to take care of a woman by listening and understanding.

Yvonne

I don't know if this theory is unique or not, but I really promote just being real in any relationship. Some people say "play hard to get" or "be mysterious" but I think it's all about not making an effort to change your personality. I guess my ultimate message is to let it all hang out. Risk everything . . . "You better bet your life."—The Who

Melissa

Si estas interesado
en ella respetela y no
jueges con sus emociones.
Si tu mejor amiga is una
muchacha presentala a
la muchacha que quieres
conquister para que no
piensemos que estas jugando
con sus emociones
                I sabel , 21 yrs,
                Palms Casino LV, NV

Respect the girl. If your
best friend is a female, properly introduce
her to the girl you like to
avoid any misunderstandings.
                Isabel

True, but even if a guy does that, unless his girlfriend is REALLY secure, he
won't be chillin' with his former bff for much longer. I'm just sayin' . . .

To EVERY guy: All you have to remember is that understanding a girl is easy!! All you have to do is keep being interested and SHOW INTEREST!!! Calling us and attempting to show us little ways you care MEANS THE WORLD!!! To know you're thinking of us!! Don't shy away!! If you're interested—let us know. We really aren't complicated at all! The GOOD girls don't play games—pick the good girls like me!!!

Christina

Men often need to get out of their own heads a bit more and give women a chance to truly connect with them. They give up on themselves and on women too soon.

Marian

Communications regarding dreams are bricks in the foundation.

Nina

Both guys and girls think they know each other. They don't! I think communication is the motherfuckin' key! No one understands how to communicate. Tell each other what you feel, and be honest. But relationships suck, so people need to understand that.

Susan, bartender

Each one of us is different and feels differently about everything. Sometimes we even feel differently day to day. If you don't understand, just ask!

Jerra

Getting a guy to ask for anything—driving directions, instructions to assemble a swing set, an update on your daily moods—isn't going to be the easiest thing in the world. Men have to swallow their pride and solicit advice from time to time.

We aren't mind readers. Communication is ESSENTIAL. TO ALL MEN: You don't just wake up and say "I want to be a good man." You must first find the good within you that has always been there...then you'll find happiness with her.

Luscious Liz Hernandez, Power 106 FM Los Angeles, "Big Boy's" Neighborhood

Men think all women want commitment, or the type of relationship that requires vast amounts of communication and time. While this is usually the case, I think more important than meeting the family or hearing the L word is respect. We understand that timing is everything and sometimes it's not punctual for commitment. That being said, if there is a simple level of respect that exists, you can probably still get laid (men also assume that they are the only ones who desire sex) and not worry about fighting. This doesn't mean that you have to open doors, walk on the appropriate side of the street, or drop your jacket over a puddle (most women have deemed chivalry passé); this just means that honesty is appreciated and recognized.

Honesty is one of the most important and rare traits of character. By simply telling the truth, you don't have to be as creative, don't have to worry about getting caught in a lie, and don't have to worry about having the conversation of clarity about the expectations. If the guidelines are clear and everyone understands the qualities of the relationship, no one gets hurt and even if you move on, or get over it, you still possess good character, something that is very rare. It is unnecessary to express fake feelings for someone. Often, women are just as scared of commitment as men and if your idea of cementing a relationship is stating falsehoods, you are confused.

One final thought: It is very bewildering why anyone would spend time with a person that they do not hold in high regard. Time is the only investment that you cannot get back, so if you are spending time with a human being in any circumstance where you feel dissatisfied, realize there are no refunds on time.

The time you spend is lost forever, never to be given back. So be a little more selective, as always it's quality, not quantity.

Your infinite source of wisdom,
Jamie Barker

There are two major moments in my life that Barker was a part of. In 2006, my grandma passed away and, as I'm sure you can understand, I was pretty devastated. Jamie came over and just sat with me while I tried to absorb what had happened. It was a simple gesture, but as anyone who has gone through something similar (and let's be honest, all of us have) knows, it meant a lot to me. Also, as my deadline for the book was upon me, she came over to offer support as I wrote away into the early morning to get it done. Mind you, she didn't do much but sleep on the couch—but it was still nice to have someone there. And after three tries at writing something for the book, she finally hit the nail on the head with this one. I strongly agree that we simply *cannot* waste the precious time that we're given in this world by spending it with people who are not deserving of our time and companionship. There are no do-overs in this life. You've gotta try to surround yourself with people who make you happy.

- Be thoughtful (this WILL earn you points in the bedroom).

- Surprise us and be bold. We will look up to your inner strengths.

- Don't assume what we're going to do or say. We're just as capable of change as you are.

- Slow dance with us, even if there's no music.

- Communicate, be direct, tell us what you want. We're smart and can handle what you have to say.

- The grass isn't always greener. Remember we're probably bored with the mundane, too.

- Be patient when we change clothes a hundred times. We know you are visual beings and only want to look great for you.

- Get over the Madonna-Whore complex. We are multitasking creatures and this unorthodox mix can take you into another dimension.

- Dare to engage us. You may be shocked at what we have up our sleeves!

Cassie

- Stop texting and pick up the effing phone and call!

- If you ask for our IM you are a loser! Ask for our number!

- We don't want you to ask for our IM and MySpace names, etc. Why? Because you can stalk us before knowing us and you can make decisions about us before we get a dinner out of it!

- Giving head is a very unselfish thing. If you meet a girl and she sucks your dick when she first meets you, chances are she's a slut. However, if you are intimate with a girl and she does it, it shows that she can get pleasure out of making you happy.

- If you're going to cheat on your girlfriend, just tell her. Don't lie to her face about it. Just say you just wanna be single.

- Sometimes we don't want to fucking cuddle.

- Say what you mean.

- If you have a big dick, don't think that's enough. You still have to work.

Laura, Lauren, and Lindsay

1) Sometimes we don't want to fucking cuddle. I agree ☺
2) Say what you mean
3) If you have a big dick, don't think that's enough. You still have to work.

We ask for your MySpace address because we've got to check out how many pics you have posted from the NBA All-Star weekend or how many backstage shots you've taken at the SCREAM tour before we decide if you're worth the boneless buffalo wings at Chili's! For real, though—nothing beats good old-fashioned face-to-face interaction when you're trying to get to know someone.

I've got a few things:

First, Never talk about your ex-girlfriends, especially things that were done in the bedroom. Its never good to compare your current girl to the ex. She's an "ex" for a reason please keep it that way!

2nd: If you've been in a relationship for a while, stop acting like a pathetic "horn dog" every damn day, like you never get any! There are times when woman like to cuddle + watch movies + know that you care for her in other ways then just relieving yourselves. Sex is great but there are times when most women are

just not in the mood or have
more on their mind then your
penis. Thirdly: Never threaten
your girl about going some where
else. If you do She should
dump your ass in 2 seconds.
& She will never trust you
after that. So keep your
'bullshit thoughts to yourself !

Danielle
dancer, choreographer,
bartender.
9/8/07

P.S. Stop trying to pick
up on bartenders
they all laugh @ you
After you leave the bar !!

PSS. By the way, Men who listen to Tom Lankis are pretty pathetic. I've been to two live showings + the men who were there were disgusting and no where near an "LA#3". If you have to listen to a 4 times divorced fat man on the radio for relationship + sexual advice "Get A LIFE" + grow up!

Another bartender and she seems kinda . . . angry . . . wouldn't ya say? Man, these girls must hear it all at work, so I can understand their frustration. It does seems like this one is directed at one person in particular, not all men in general. Whew, what a relief!!

money

her looks

P.M.S

a man that
doesn't make her feel
attractive.

CHAPTER 4

RESPECT

Respect, as you have already read in some of the previous entries, is very important in a relationship. Without it, the coupling is doomed to fail. Does respect mean putting that other person up on a pedestal? Does respect mean giving in to someone's every wish and whim? I'll leave it up to you to find an exact definition, but one way or another, respect is clearly essential. And if you're still having trouble getting it, just listen to Aretha—she'll break it down for ya.

I feel that every man should respect a woman the way they respect their mother.

Chameir

I hate that men try to front and play it off when they feel/care/love a female. They let their pride get in their way. I cannot stand industry men for that reason because they always treat women like they're less just because of their status, money, or fame. Respect women, love them, embrace them. We're the mothers of the earth.

Fabiola

FYI: The "industry" that Fabiola is referring to is the entertainment field—actors, producers, musicians, etc.

It seems that men and women will always remain the same in terms of the fact that they'll never fully understand each other. For instance, why do men walk so far ahead of you, only to have to wait for you anyway at that particular destination? Also, never look for a ten—there isn't one. But you can love a six who can be a ten one day and a zero the next. Spoken from a married woman. Twenty-eight years!!

Jasmine

Don't try too hard to get with a woman. If she wants you she'll let you know some way, somehow. Respect a woman even when fighting. An overprotective man leads to a mischievous woman.

Karla

Patty - 24 -
morning show
assistant ~~ass~~ producer

~~firsts~~ girss

DO

T-ART!

So much for her blaming the dog!

Just treat me right.

Emily

> Chubb Rock told me that back in 1990.

For starters... Men *must* understand they must never slip out of a woman's bed in the middle of the night!! Unless perhaps there is a fire drill... a flood... or an earthquake! Tell a woman she is beautiful... tell a woman you love her... only if you do!!! Be honest! Be realistic!! Be who you always strive to be...

"Green Eyes" by Coldplay makes an enormous impact.

P.S.   IT'S OKAY TO CRY!!

Beth

Listen up, men. You can get away with a bit of naughty behavior if you just make sure you're giving your special lady consistent good loving. It makes us feel more connected and provides you with a longer leash.

Denise

Denise and I crossed paths while standing in a taxi line outside of the Palms Hotel in Vegas. I had just wrapped up a three-day shoot for an MTV project there and was heading home. I ran in and used the bathroom before we left and told everyone to hold on because I'd be right back. We had two taxis to the airport and I guess everyone in the first cab thought I was in the second and everyone in the second thought I was in the first. They were both wrong. I stepped back outside to find that everyone had rolled out, and I had to find my own ride. Enter Denise. We shared a ride to the airport and in the fifteen-or-so-minute trip I pulled out the book, explained it to her, and had her write an entry. Quick work by yours truly!

I grew up in a strict Catholic family of nine kids. Sex was never discussed. I wanted my boys to understand love, sex, and the difference between them. What they see on MTV, movies, etc. is not reality. I explained to them at a young age the menstrual process that girls go through—hoping they would be more sensitive to their girlfriends' mood swings, and girls in general. I believe I achieved my goal—they have grown to be responsible and caring young men. When I think about those discussions (we discussed more subjects as time went on—herpes, chlamydia, cramps, Midol)—they are what brought us closer as friends and confidants.

Patti, mother of three boys—fifteen,
seventeen, and twenty-one; married twenty-four years

Most parents aren't comfortable enough with themselves to have these types of discussions with their kids, so I commend Patti for being able to do so. And I'm pretty sure her sons have benefited from being so well-informed about girls, and from a good source—unlike most of us, who learned most of what we know from watching a scrambled version of *Bachelor Party* on late-night TV . . .

Everything men understand about women? Nothing . . .

All I can do is raise my son to respect women and to be decent, to find the beauty within and to embrace it, to communicate and to be vulnerable . . . Luckily for me and my son, he will be raised by strong women who will teach him strength. He will be allowed in the inner circle and for this he will be better off.

Robin

There are women out there you can't have; don't take it personally. A woman, by nature, wants a man (unless we're talking about lesbians), but for this exercise—yes, women WANT a man who is/does what she needs—but she doesn't always need it. Let's take me, for instance—a man could bring me love, kindness, companionship, money, eternity, children . . . and there is a chance I'd still say no, it's just not going to happen. So accept if a woman doesn't want it and stop taking it personal—because it's not about you, love, you're an angel. I promise some other time.

Adrienne

DON'T PLAY GAMES! Be honest and up front (with respect, of course). This way you'll get where you're going a lot quicker.

Heather

Honesty is such a lonely word. Heather's right—the truth shall set you free. At least when you're up front with your intentions you can avoid dragging out a situation that wasn't going to work in your favor in the first place. But games *can* be fun, especially if the game is Twister or Spin the Bottle or a little thing I like to call Just the Tip . . . ya know, I'll stop right there.

To all the wonderful men of God . . .

What you do will always be louder than what you say.

Faune

Don't be "Mr. McFeely" when you just meet a lady! :)

Melinda, RN, Super Bowl XLII Sunday!

I was supposed to go to the Super Bowl with my boy Matt, but he got sick the night before and couldn't make it. He told me if I didn't sell the tickets (which both of us wanted to do since neither my team, the Cowboys, nor his team, the Steelers, was in the game) he was gonna give his to his high school friend Melinda. I decided not to scalp the tickets—not because I suddenly had a guilty conscience, but because by the time I physically had the tickets in my hand, kickoff was only thirty-five minutes away and there just wasn't enough time. So Melinda made it in the beginning of the second quarter and although I was worried about having to watch the game with a girl I'd never met before—my worry was that I'd have to explain everything that was going on—I was very surprised by her knowledge of football. (It shouldn't have surprised me, though—I think most women from Pennsylvania have some grasp of the game.) Sometime during the third quarter I told her about the book and she wrote her entry. It was kind of funny that even with the excitement of a Super Bowl on the line, I kept this book in mind.

A woman who spends lots of money to enhance their looks, gives more value to it instead of their (her) inner selve(s). Don't place her worth on her looks! She may be covering up and or masking whats really going on inside. True beauty comes from the softness of a womans heart and the rest always follows.

L. Mabry
Feb 7, 2008
49 yrs old
Manager / Philanthropist

Some basic rules that women like:

1.   Always hold the door.

2.   Always pull out the chair.

3.   Always be a gentleman. No matter how much money you make, no matter what you do for a living, kindness will get you everywhere!

Amy, mother of two boys (to whom I will teach this knowledge)

I met Amy Kates and her husband, David, earlier in the day that she wrote in the journal. I had the good fortune to be on the Turks and Caicos Islands, and I had taken a golf cart for a spin. I wound up getting the cart stuck in some really soft sand, and every time I hit the gas the tires would spin and sink the cart farther. Enter David and Amy, who happened to be walking by. David offered his help and hatched a plan. Simply pushing the cart wouldn't do because of how far it had sunk into the sand. David set off on a hunt for a piece of wood that he had seen earlier in the day near the same spot. As he scrambled around looking for it Amy smiled and shook her head and told me that I was lucky that Dave had seen me: "He lives for doing stuff like this." David found the wooden plank and got back to the cart at the same moment a security guard was pulling up to tow me out, but after all of our efforts to move the cart, David was gonna be damned if he let the guard come to the rescue without at least giving it one more try. We lifted up the cart and placed the hunk of wood under the tire and . . . Well, despite our best MacGyver-like efforts we didn't succeed and the security cart had to pull my cart out. David, Amy, and I ran into one another later that night at the hotel bar and I got Amy to share her thoughts. To the young Kates men—listen to your mom when she tells you these things . . . It's not always easy being a gentleman, and many times in life you'll shake your head in disbelief when you see girls/women with the biggest assholes you've ever met. But in the long run, you'll be better men and the type of women you want *will* notice.

Always treat her as though she's important to you. Listen to her. Pay attention to the little things. Realize she notices everything. Be honest and open. Do things just to make her smile. It's all right to show emotion and be vulnerable. We're attracted to it. We want to feel close to you and for you to feel comfortable telling us things.

Emily

yevette (25)

남자친구랑 슈포7갔다

남자친구가 쩌쩔중냈다..

여자늘 딿으라고생가녀ㅇ

늘남자친구 !!

a lot of Men try to
undermine women,
thinking if they Make her
feel bad about herself,
She'll be grateful to have
that man—that no one
else will want her. Bottom
line, No woman WAnts
to fuck a man that
doesn't make her feel
attractive. Men fantasize
about us. We fantasize
about Men fantasizing
about us.

Suzy McCoppen— 30
Journalist 3/20/08

And yet so many women stay with men who treat them like crap. So what she says here sounds good in theory, but I kind of disagree. It seems like some women want to be with a man who treats them poorly because they want to be the one who tames him. Good luck with that! It's one thing to be drawn to a bad boy that rides Harleys, is all tatted up, raps for Diddy, or plays for the Detroit Pistons. It's a whole other story when she falls for a man that subjects her to mental or physical abuse. This may be the one time I stand on a soapbox to scold my fellow man, but guys—let's knock that shit off. If you're not meant to be together, then move on. Screwing with her mind or, god forbid, hitting her is cowardly and will not make her love you.

Fellas, Suzy is *Playboy*'s Party Girl. You can check out her work on their website. And if you're a fan of Cowgirls, may I suggest *Entourage* season 1, episode 8 . . . you're welcome!

Okay, here it goes . . .

Be careful what you do, be careful what you say.

There are certain monumental moments a man has control of. Making a commitment, getting engaged, moving in, getting married. As children boys play with guns, action figures, and violent video games and are "toughened up." Little girls play with baby dolls that piss and shit, and fake kitchens, and they play house. By the time a chick reaches her twenties she's spent the majority of her life essentially in training to be a girlfriend, wife, mother. Men are still in "me mode" in their twenties. From the moment you show interest in a woman she isn't thinking "I can't wait to hang out again, he seems nice." She's thinking "Is he the one for me? Can this go somewhere? Is he ready for something real?" Women are nesters. Men are procreators. Men often feel a certain amount of pressure in the first several months of a relationship. Let me fill you in on what's going on inside of a woman at this time. "Is he a bullshitter? Is he going to be as big of a douchebag as the last guy? Should we sleep together yet? Is he seeing other women?" Men are always escaping the noose once those telltale signs start creeping in to what used to be a fun, pressure-free hangout/makeout session. Women want to be committed, which generally seems to be the polar opposite of what men want. The dilemma lies in how men go about getting what they want. If all you want to do is fuck, then tell a girl so she at least can make the decision of whether she wants to honestly do that or not. Don't start filling her head with delusions of grandeur about how your kids are going to look, future vacations, and decorating tastes for your future hypothetical home because it's just wrong and a woman's emotions shouldn't be fucked with. Men wonder why women turn psycho, there is your answer. Show me a woman a man claims is psycho, sit her in a room to get her half of the story, and Mr. Spic and Span will have shit all over his hands. Women can handle the truth, and we'll respect you for it.

Mia

Lesson #1
Tell the truth, women can handle the truth over a lie! Don't be SCARED!

Lesson #2
Take the time to find out how each woman you are with likes it. What works for I may not work for another.

Lesson #3
When a girl says she doesn't like another girl AGREE with her! She's saying it for a reason!

Lesson #4
We like to "FUCK" so quit using that bullshit excuse that you're tired of being with the same woman! That's a cop-out and we're too smart to full for that crap!

Lesson #5

P.M.S. is REAL! We don't wanna be cranky, so just deal with it, and don't complain about it.

lesson #6

LISTEN! We don't talk just to hear ourselves even though you might think that's the case.

This lesson was brought to you by:

Launa

on:

6.6.06

(Kinda creepy date!)

Fellas, listen up. Lesson 3 is the easiest way possible to earn points with a girl, and you really don't have to do anything but nod your head in approval and keep it moving. And it keeps her off your back while you watch *Friday* for the thirty-fifth time.

Now, in regard to Lesson 1 . . . A lot of women wrote something along the lines of "We can handle the truth," which instantly brings to mind the vision of Jack Nicholson in *A Few Good Men* screaming at Tom Cruise, "YOU *CAN'T* HANDLE THE TRUTH!" For example: Girls, you know when you squeeze, and I mean realllly squuuuuuuueeeeze, into your favorite pair of jeans that you bought three years ago, the ones you can't fit into without help from a friend to pull them up . . . THOSE JEANS? Now, when you ask us, "Do these make me look fat?" think about whether or not you can handle the truth over a lie. Because some things are better left unsaid!

No matter what you
think, you don't know
anything about women.

#1) we are always right

#2) you should always know
what we really know

#3) were the Best

#4 u bestere worshipus?

#5) spoil us like no
other :) 11/26/04
Katy & April

***Okay, T. J., so that was apparently how I feel when I am wasted. But here are my thoughts sober. You can include either or both. It's up to you.

1) Don't tell us anything unless you really mean it. It will just get you into trouble in the future.

2) Always behave like a gentleman.

3) Tell us we look beautiful from time to time.

4) Show us affection in public sometimes, but it doesn't have to be in front of "the boys."

5) We do love gifts . . . hint hint ;-) . . . handbags are a good one!!

Kelly

Again, there is some conflict here with #1 . . . I always say, don't ask a question if you don't really want to know the answer.

Jessica   3/4/07

Respect and cherish her!
Also, fuck her good and hard
as much as she wants it.
Don't forget to eat it first though.
:)

Don't play games... that's
lame.
Have patience w/her through her
emotional rollercoasters. That's just
the way women are. Deal w/it!

I just smile when I read this!

11·26·2007

Open doors for your
date !! Don't stick
your tongue in her
ears EVER ... AND if
she is a Playboy Bunny
Don't grab her Bunny
tail. AND DON'T EVER
Hit on your dates
friends 'cuz if she
catches you, your
Name is MUDD...
    FUNNy BUNNy LOVE
    AND LAUGHTER

Julie McCullough
        X ♡ X

Julie was *Playboy*'s Miss February 1986 and starred on *Growing Pains* for a
season as the girlfriend of a personal hero of mine growing up—Mike Seaver.
Most teenage boys (and, let's face it, grown men) had a crush on her at that
time—and one on Denise Huxtable, who sadly does not appear in this book.

What men need to know:

- Not every woman has PMS.

- Many women could just be sensitive, not a bitch.

- Most women want to be motherly and take care of someone—it's a natural instinct. Men should take advantage—appreciate it.

- Men take all the many abilities of women for granted—birth, monthly sensitivity—bear with it—it's for a man!

- In society today women struggle with many insecurities—it's a continuous challenge for us. Men, if you have a woman, realize she is doing everything—being cute, new outfits, reading magazines on sex and fashion, manicures and pedicures, waxing, even "pineapple juice"—LOL—all for you. It's a constant society pressure to please a man. Don't take it for granted—embrace it. So it doesn't hit you in the face when your woman, your mother, your sister realizes that is what you are doing. Be conscious of every woman's action . . . We deal with a lot more than men see—just pay more attention! Women have their own team they take care of and coach every play along the way called life. Men and Women—it's a team companionship—EMBRACE!

Whitney

Thanks to my girl Donna D. (Chi-Town stand-up) for explaining the mystery of "pineapple juice" to me. She informed me that—and I'm not sure if this is an old wives' tale or not—if you drink pineapple juice it makes your . . . your . . . ahh . . . It gives a better taste to your . . . It gives the berries a sweeter juice . . . Look, we're all adults here, you know what the hell I'm talking about.

stop

dicking around

women need a hug.

Yes Dear

keep it

short.

CHAPTER 5

LISTENING

A man's attention span is usually about fifteen minutes . . . Go!

Ha ha. Funny, right? Seriously, though, I separated these contributions out from the communication chapter for a reason. Yes, being a good listener is part of being a good communicator, but as you'll read, men seem to have a real problem listening when it comes to simple stuff—not just complicated relationship stuff. Like when she asks you to go to the grocery store. Some guys find themselves aimlessly wandering the aisles, having forgotten what they were supposed to buy. Nothing will make her madder quicker than you calling and asking what you were supposed to buy. Nothing, except *not* buying what it was that she wanted you to buy. Pay attention, because if you bring home three lemons when baby wanted twelve, you are in for it. Open

your ears, men, to even the small stuff. It will make your ladies much happier. But

don't take it from me. Take it from the words that follow.

Listen to what we are saying to you! Do you understand the words that are coming out of my mouth?!? Just LISTEN! And try to be a little more sensitive! Thanks.

Becky

Stop yelling and just listen—and always make her blush.

Claire

Listen to us—about our day or something we're going through. Let us vent and be there to offer advice then snap us out of it. Make us laugh, and suddenly whatever it was that was bothering us doesn't bother us anymore. And when we fight, understand where we are coming from and we'll do the same thing. Make fun of us in a funny way, and whatever we were fighting about, we won't remember anymore.

All men are different, of course, so it's hard to answer the "What do they do right/wrong?" question. But I can answer what I like and what I am attracted to. I love a guy who listens to me, who understands how I am feeling and just gets me. I love a guy who is not afraid to be open. Who speaks his mind even if he thinks it's corny. I love corny. I love mush. I love a man who has that vulnerable side but at the same time also has that male protector instinct. I feel safe with him and he brings out the best in me . . . being with him makes me overall a better person.

I would say to all men to be yourselves—there is a woman out there who will love you for who you are, exactly how you are. Don't try to be something that you're not just to win the girl. And, girls, same goes for you. I think each person knows emotionally what they want out of a relationship—so don't settle for anything less. Lastly, honesty and sincerity go a long way. Respect us and we will respect you back.

Play games, and that is when we get complicated because you are not being real and we sense that.

Ashley Alexandra Dupré

Hi! Guys, listen to a woman when she has something to say! It makes the relationship so much easier. Make her feel special every day and she will give you all her love.

Hordana

Men, remember little things women tell you!! Make a reservation, call when you say you are going to call, remember a birthday, a wedding date. When women are talking, pay attention. If you are not paying attention and are distracted by something else, say so!! As much as we love to talk, we want someone to listen.

Lexie

Men need to learn to listen with an open heart to the words coming out of our mouths. When women vent that doesn't mean we want a man's "pearls of wisdom"—we just want to be listened to and heard.

Anonymous

When a woman is upset and wants to vent about whatever—her job, demanding boss, or unruly hair—her man needs to lay back, be supportive, and listen. A little silence and agreeable head nodding can go a long, long way for him.

Ashleigh

Silence and head nodding can also be achieved while napping ;-)

5/12/07

Män försöker lösa
problem... Allt kvinnor
behöver är en kram.

Hanna (Örebro, Sweden)

TRANSLATION:

When a woman is telling her man about something that is bothering her—she isn't asking for a solution. She is just looking for comfort and a hug.

Hanna from Sweden

Women are all different. What may make one woman cry can make another laugh. A man should pay attention in order to understand a lady. I'm not saying that we always make sense. Most of us are emotional creatures, and we act from our hearts. In any case, every HUMAN'S desire is to be heard and understood, so listen up! (Even if you don't really get it.) Speaking personally, I can say that a good listener and someone who has ideas and can share them is ideal. Communication is paramount. I believe that women talk to express themselves and men express themselves through action. When men communicate through talking and women put action behind their words, we can really build something lasting and important. Are you even listening to me?

xoxo, Mecca

Huh, what's that?!? Were you saying something?

What men need to know is pretty simple; if you can listen and be consistent, you're in! We can be confusing, and one woman might do whatever you want and always be here for you and another might have no time for you. And you might feel that way about two girls. The key is going out and finding the girl who feels the same as you. Don't force it. That will only lead to pain! Be honest even if it hurts because it will only save you a worse hurt later! Give in—give backrubs, give lots of kisses and flowers! Tell her she is beautiful and have surprise sex a lot!

Bijou Phillips

Chances are, guys will only pay attention to the surprise-sex part.

May 1, 2007 (midnight) (16 days to my

Dr. Better Man —

Here's the deal. Gonna give it to you straight and

simple . . .

1. Treat your would woman the way you ^want your mother or sister to be treated.

2. Learn how to eat pussy . . . I mean, be a master of your craft

31st B.Day So listen up!)

3. Pay just a little more
fucking attention. I know
I gotta keep it short.
But stop dicking around
when I'm talking to you.

XOXO,
    Jen Avina (divorced)
producer / Enlighter / Bad-Ass

P.S. When all else fails just
say 'yes Dear' even if you are
        right. Trust me (you don't have
to mean it.)

Always listen and pay attention. Make us feel like the most beautiful woman in the world—we want to feel irresistible, so compliment us often! Women have a tendency to talk a lot, so just listen and let us vent. We want to feel protected. Be supportive of choices that we make and give constructive advice. Don't be a pushover, and definitely don't let us take advantage—it's not attractive! Be yourself and don't tell us lies! We CAN handle the truth! Treat us like the beautiful creatures that we are and rock our world in the bedroom!

Tracy

- Remember all important dates, even if they seem insignificant to you.

- Always listen with full attention and respond and remember the conversation a month later. Absorb the information.

- Compliment the small things.

- Take notice of everything.

- Honesty is best, always.

- We need romance!!! Don't forget to KISS. Make out like when you were in high school.

- Don't be afraid to show you give a shit. LOL :)

Claudia

Tongue all down your throat, too much spit, awkward groping, octopus arms coming at ya in all directions . . . Do you really want us to make out like we did in high school?

lie.

we know
before may
not i do

truth
might
hurt,

CHAPTER 6

HONESTY

As you'll find in the following pages, women seem to just want honesty in their relationships. Most claim that they want to know the real deal. In my experience, that isn't always true. But read on and judge for yourselves.

Men need to be completely honest. Don't say "I like you" just because I said it first. Be honest, and if you don't like that person the same way, tell them so. Don't sugarcoat it just to benefit your own needs. Don't be selfish, and respect the feelings of the person that cares for you. And if you can't do that, expect to never be fulfilled entirely with your heart's desires.

Sarah

Don't try to fool us because we know.

Lea DiPerna

Lea is my accountant . . . So, yeah, she's definitely one person I can't fool.

Las mujeres prefieren Honestidad sobre qualquier cosa! La Honestidad es una Virtud! Aunque la verdad duela, siempre te mantendra libre. Yo prefiero llorar sobre una verdad que llorar sobre una mentira!

♡! mirtha
June 2nd 2007

TRANSLATION:

Women prefer honesty over anything else! Honesty is a virtue! Even though the truth might hurt, it will always set you free. I prefer to cry over a truth than over a lie!

Mirtha

Men need to understand
one thing about women.
We know EVERYTHING you
do! Men think they are
so sneaky and just
because women might
play dumb, they think
that they got away with
something. But guess
what? You are wrong!
⊛Aside from "A woman's
intution", we are investigators
We practically know what
you're going to do before you
do it. So just keep that in
the back of your mind.
                    11-16-06 MS. FORD

This is a recurring theme throughout the book—women thinking they know everything—but I beg to differ. I once told a girl I met at a club that I was an astronaut, and another one that I invented the search engine Ask Jeeves, and they both believed me. Maybe they were just playing dumb?

Keep your word. When you say you're gonna do something, DO IT! PLAIN AND SIMPLE! It's not hard to make a girl happy. Just listen, DON'T break her heart, don't lie, don't cheat, don't say things just because it's what she wants to hear. Be honest! Love the ones who treat you right! Forget the ones who don't! Bottom line, don't let me down! One love.

Jen F.

This is just my personal opinion: When it comes to cheating (and this goes both ways) I believe you should NEVER tell! If you are truly unhappy in a relationship and you do cheat, let the woman go!! If you love her and believe your cheating was a mistake, keep it to yourself!! DO NOT try to absolve yourself of your guilt by telling her what you did!! It will only hurt her, and if you are the man you should be, you wouldn't want her to feel pain for your mistake!

Tracey

But wouldn't it hurt more if you just left her without giving a reason? It seems to me that this would be a lot more harmful than just fessing up and coming clean.

Seriously, all that I really want—just an honest and faithful, romantic guy. Someone that's understanding and loyal. Just a faithful mo-fo. (Sorry for being a little ghetto.) But someone that can understand where I'm coming from, who's not jealous and insecure.

Farhat

Geena the Latina
11-22-06

- Men need to understand that a woman just wants to be loved
- a hug is better than a kiss sometimes
- when we R in a bad mood - just let us be in a bad mood
- tell us we R beautiful - even when we say we R ugly
- if we ever say "Do I look fat" Always say NO!!

Geena is a friend of mine, and a morning radio personality in San Diego. She supported this project long before it was a finished product, and I'm really grateful to her for it.

1. Always compliment the girl.

2. Don't be too eager—it's a turnoff!

3. Play hard to get, but still give her attention.

4. DON'T LIE. We always find out and we'll never trust you again.

5. Get your fun out of your system before you settle!

Lia

"Get your fun outta your system before you settle!" Finally, someone said it. It's really one of the biggest fears men have with relationships—the thought that settling down is a death sentence for fun. And I'm sure there are many women out there who feel the exact same way. Both people have to make sure their bond stays fresh, exciting, and fun, or else the other problems will, without a doubt, start to surface.

What do men need to know? You will not get away with it. We will find out everything and use whatever resources we can to catch you in a lie. Your e-mail password? We know it. Your MySpace password? We know it. Any and every text and phone call on your phone? We've seen it. We've got friends everywhere and they will never be on your side. Sorry. If you want to be sneaky, then date a guy. We are sneakier. Also, it is NEVER okay to hang out with an ex-girlfriend. And we NEVER want to be their friend. We aren't psycho and we do trust you. It's the girl we don't trust. I don't want to be around the two of you together—ever. We'll only think about and picture you two together. If you want to hang out with an ex, you will not be hanging out with me . . . at all. And invite us even if you don't want us there. We know when you want to have alone time—so we'll probably say "No, you go ahead" anyway. But not inviting us will only make us mad.

P.S.   We like it rough.

Gina

If I'm not mistaken, Gina had just broken up with her boyfriend. I found that when girls had recently become single they had a *lot* on their minds and loved sharing those thoughts. She hits the nail on the head with most of this, so, men, pay extra-close attention. Re-read it and commit it to memory if need be. It's gonna keep you out of a lot of trouble. She definitely laid it down quite flat, but after the scolding she was nice enough toss in that insight about how women like it rough. That makes the scolding a lot easier to take.

Call when you say you will. Be honest. Listen! Be creative (in bed and out!). If you want to cheat it means the relationship is bad, so end it before you cheat! Say "I love you!" often, but only if you mean it. Avoid using the word *crazy*. Men tend to throw this word out when fighting and the results are never good. Go out with the guys and make sure your girl goes out with her friends. Having your own lives is very important. Communicate!

Tami

never get

used

to it

handing me
Ben and Jerrys

dont

never get used to it handing me Ben and Jerrys / dont /

CHAPTER 7

PMS

My boy Travis aka Lover T was talking about PMS as I was working on this chapter, so I decided to let his voice be heard.

"The first three days of [my girl's] PMS are the worst of my life. Now, I know I'll never go through the things a woman does, but for those first couple of days . . . Man, she says some of the meanest things I've ever heard. After those days pass, the meanness is gone but then she is just grumpy, which I can deal with. But those first three days . . . WOW."

Here women tell men how it really feels to have PMS, so we men can really understand. I think that this is the most important chapter in the book. Heed these words, men. They may be the most relevant you find in these pages.

Once a month, I get to bitch unconditionally about whatever I deem necessary, and for any duration I may choose. Any solutions offered on your behalf pertaining to these matters will be not only unwelcome but rejected. Please bear in mind that the occasional “uh-huh, exactly” will be silently noted for appreciation at a later date.

C. Henry

Casey

Sometimes when I'm
venting about something
I don't want a solution
I just wanna get it
out... and you need
to just listen!

Around every 28-32 days you should tell me that I'm pretty, and skinny while simultaneously handing me a pint of Ben and Jerrys Cherry Garcia Ice Cream.

-Sarah

I've gotta say, this may be my favorite entry, but I wondered why she chose to use twenty-eight to thirty-two days. It didn't make sense to me. Then a girl pointed out that that was the menstrual cycle . . . Derrrrr, that never even occurred to me.

In all actuality you know can't live without us. If you want the sex, then deal with our bitchy, cranky mood swings, and then at the end of the day we're both happy. Grin and bear it. You know you love us!

Susanne

Now, if the bitchy, cranky mood swings were all guys had to deal with, that would be great, but it's more than that . . . So, so much more.

When women are grumpy it's not PMS! Well, not all the time. :)

Amelia

So when it isn't PMS you are just grumpy? I figured as much. Ladies, Amelia has just spilled the beans on you.

I met Amelia at the Logan Valley Mall in Altoona, Pennsylvania. She was in Waldenbooks and happened to be standing in the section where you'd find the relationship books. I saw her looking through a few of them so I figured I had a great in to get her involved, and it would make for a good story. Which I just shared with you.

1   Barking at a girl will NEVER get you a hookup, date, etc.

2   Girls love attention, so make her feel special.

3   Having your "bro" speak to a girl for you will get you nowhere!!!

4   Respect a woman's independence and intelligence—it shows security in a man.

5   Never ask a woman if it's that time of the month!

6   One more thing—a piece of paper is not necessary to make something real. Be true to your girl and she'll be true to you! Be honest—that's all!

Heather

partner, tie you down

not prison,

give me some notice on I'm booked

CHAPTER 8

SPACE

The best way to lose someone you love is to smother them. Most of us have agendas and things we need to get done, so we don't always want someone in our pockets 24/7. *Everyone needs a chance to breathe and keep a bit of their individuality.* After all, isn't that what attracted you to them in the first place? Here, women make themselves clear— they don't always want to "mommy" their men. They need their space, too.

..men need to understand, every girl is different, not all of us want to tie you down, we want space too.

• javonna

P.S.
periods are the worst you can never get used to it, feel 4 us.

This could have easily appeared in the previous chapter. It seems that periods and PMS are such an issue that women feel the need to mention them often. That said, I felt like Javonna's message that women need space, too, was the more important thing here.

If we're going somewhere and I'm rushing to get ready, stop saying "Hurry up!" It only makes me mess up my eyeliner and have to do it again, which takes us longer to leave. Relax, I know we have to go.

Tigra

The Lady Tigra was one half of the late-eighties hip-hop group L'Trimm. Her advice is right on point—unless she's running *super* late, there is no reason to rush her while she is beautifying herself for you. I'm sure the finished product will be well worth the wait.

MEN! Listen up!

Women are organized social
creatures. Don't call
me w/ 20 minutes notice
to grab a drink or food.
I am always booked so
if you want to go out on
a date give me some
notice. Also - quit
playing the phone game!

-Katie
JUNE 14, 2007

Give them their space! Have fun! Don't get too serious too fast! Make them laugh! Open the door! Make friends with her parents. Give her SPACE!!! Jealousy is a BADDD thing! Kiss her forehead!

Hunter

Don't call continuously. Girls like their space just as much as guys. Calm and respectful is the best attitude possible. Jealousy encourages a girl to do "bad" things. Indifference can be intriguing. Believe me—I married an "indifferent" man!

Angela

I don't know what I should
understand about all ?.
I do know that what I
need to understand about
me is that I am about
being a partner, not a
symbol of a prison - partners
allow the other to be who
they are ... Really ... with
all flaws + perfections.
Love is something that continuously
grows + expands, is not limiting
+ is the truth of who
all humans are - no
matter ~~which~~ which sex
they happen to have been
born into.

Heather

1. Every girl needs her space.

2. Girls think about sex more than you think.

3. Why do men have fantasies about girl-on-girl action? I don't understand.

4. A way to a girl's heart is humor.

Nikki

Let me try to help ya get a firm grasp on 3, Nikki. Imagine coming home from work to find a package with a note telling you that you'd won a contest. After opening the parcel and digging through the Styrofoam peanuts, you find a brand-new pair of Christian Louboutin heels. In your size. They won't be in stores for another five months. They are all yours. Then you dig deeper in the box and find ANOTHER pair in a different style. You know that feeling of excitement that you'd have? Well, it's something like that. Ya dig?

CHAPTER 9

WOMEN ARE COMPLICATED

This truth is why this whole book came about, more or less. Men always say that we don't get women, that we don't understand them. I'm hoping *That's What She Said* will bridge the gap and make both sexes a little less complex. Here, women talk about themselves and their sometimes puzzling behaviors.

We're not that complicated!!! Some of us are just crazy!

Leslie

And a lot of you are both complicated *and* crazy. Finishing a Rubik's Cube blindfolded is less complex than figuring out women.

Carolina "Nina" 3/10/07

when a female asks to leave
her alone... that means:

Leave her Alone for 10 min?!
a let her come around!

Trust ME this
will never fail!!

(˘‿˘)

Pay close attention to this one, fellas, because it really works in our favor.
Give her all the time in the world to be pissy, and take the quiet time to sneak
in a few extra quarters of *Madden* on the Xbox. It's a win-win situation!

12/05/07
D M Y

לויד ספי

בעשרה שהגן איכה עבר
ביית עשרות נעשים נתן
אישה, אני היה עוד - נפתח
ולמה יוצאת אל זה.

היה בבית ישמע מידתך עם
המיוחד רבא אל עניין הו
את - עיתון עד ישוא לעין
מפי ראות.

דוד ישא אל להתא
באשם, רבאה אמא ושימו
כמה ועתה של בית ישימש
את נוח בעיון יא נשאם
שלי הישא דביה הנישאים

Linor Shefer 05-12-07

In order to understand
a woman, a man has
to learn to think like
a woman. He has
to learn what she
like to hear, and to
use it. He has to
have some spice in
him to give her a
litlbit space, but not
to much. He has to be
understanding, that way
she will open up to him
and He will learn more about her.

Um, let's see . . . Please let us women have freedom to go out with our friends and don't show up and stalk us. And please allow us to be the free spirits that we are and just love us and don't try too hard to understand us.

Sofia

"Don't try too hard to understand us." Sofia has given probably the best advice in the book!

"The more simpler you pick 'em, the simpler it will be"—meaning simple girls will make it easier and better to be with.

J.D.

A simple girl? Does such a thing exist?

What you need to know is not something that you can read in this book or anything I can tell you. INTUITION.

Gina

But by all means, please still buy this book.

In the way that women have become more like men, men should become more like women. No boxes.

Ilona

WHAT?!? Does this mean I get to eat Cherry Garcia and be grumpy every twenty-eight to thirty-two days, too?

Jessica aka Phwez   1/2/07

says:

Stop trying to understand Bitches. We're all Different. Learn how to handle your bitch & leave it at that.

I can't argue with this one. And it would make a great rap song.

It's difficult to write about what men understand about women because I am not aware of any men that have actually understood much about women . . . Wait, I can't speak for women in general because I'm sure that the "typical woman" is pretty easy to understand. Hmm . . . let me change my perspective. If I were a man, this is what I would ultimately understand about the opposite sex (I'll preface this by saying I am not a part of this category . . . to be explained later). Women are stubborn. They want what they can't have. They seek status. They long for someone to take care of them. They are repulsive. They are ignorant. Often obnoxious, they long for attention. They are catty and superficial. They want you to take them shopping. They lack substance. They are vapid and unaware that the actual "quality" men know what they are up to, are despised by them, but appeal to their warped little minds to get them into bed. After that night, the intelligent man will no longer speak to the above stated woman because he actually DOES know what the majority are all about. Fuck me for saying this, but most men really DO understand EVERYTHING about the "typical" woman. Hence the reason for the bold gender line and the stereotypical statement that "men are pigs." Now, in my opinion, once a quality man finds the RARE quality woman, there will be no need for "understanding" the opposite gender. If a man actually holds out and doesn't settle for the typical woman, he will eventually meet a person who is on his level. The two will have no need for self-help books on "what to do" with a man/woman—thoughts not analyzed—the real man and woman will appreciate each other for what and who they are—and fuck it up because human nature proves that once things make sense and fit perfectly we long for chaos; we miss the drama; it's all a roundabout and too common a situation of basically fucking up a good thing. Human understanding is rarely accomplished—I could write for days. Let's talk instead.

Crystal

This is pretty deep, and Crystal touches on many relevant points while depicting what she calls the "typical woman." But in your defense, ladies, while a lot of your sisters are looking in the mirror right now knowing that they've been put on blast, this is not an accurate description of women as a whole.

I also take from this that Crystal feels that no matter what, relationships are doomed to fail. Which begs the question, why even bother? But hey, the rules of the game here were to let women speak their minds, and from their hearts. So be it.

Maui girls are the best! No matter what!

April

> But the best at what? Connect 4? Tonk? Cee-Lo? The Longbow? The Plow?
> The Jet Jiggy? The Sidedish? The Underdog? At doing taxes? If so, we *really*
> need to talk.

Women are just like men, just more emotional! GET USED TO IT!

Braidy

Remind us that a relationship can only exist between two people. It can't be tried in the court of "girlfriend" opinion. Sometimes we need to be reminded that a little more talking it through with **YOU** and a little less working it out with our girls goes a long way to a healthier relationship.

Joan Morgan, author of *When Chickenheads Come Home to Roost*

This is definitely good advice. Women do tend to elicit opinions from their friends a little too much when faced with problems with their men, whereas guys don't really call up their boys for an emergency get-together to talk about their shorties. All women seem to have that angry yak of a friend who stays in her ear, telling her that her man is good for nothing. That girl has probably been single since all five original members of New Edition were together.

I'd say try working your problems out with your significant other before airing your dirty laundry in the street—like my grandma used to say, "Your business ain't everybody's business!"

Don't be blind to a woman's blatant ignorance. Ignorance may be bliss but should never be dismissed. Very often to manipulate a situation, a smart woman who knows what she wants will act a part to make sure she is in control of her desired objective. This is when a man needs to think with the brain upstairs to avoid being taken advantage of emotionally, mentally, and possibly physically.

Dawn

Thinking with the brain upstairs? No wonder we can't figure women out. This just goes to show that maybe women are a bit smarter than men.

The biggest thing men don't know about women is that every time they want to be left alone we want to be held, and when they want to be comforted we want to be left alone.

Goldman

I believe men understand us perfectly; it's human nature to use this excuse for conflict. But in the end, I feel it's in our best interest to keep men thinking we have no clue what we want. ☺

Amy Jo

I think men are misunderstood for the most part. I've spent time examining relationships and men . . . and I've discovered 98 percent of men are the same, which is in all honesty the same way women should be—open-minded and content with the fact that there is more out there. Relationships would be ideal if people would remember the fact that men will cheat and sometimes women will also! It's not a bad thing if it's honest. I feel sorry when my girlfriends are sad because their man is speaking to another woman or glances at another. I'll always be their shoulder, but I also understand the man's point of view. How many women are there out there? The chances of two people coming together that are also "soul mates" is ridiculous.

Krystal

I agree with Krystal—there are more than SIX BILLION humans on Earth, and we're to believe that there is only *one* person out there for us? I think there are probably thousands of people out there that are Mr. or Ms. Right for each of us. The goal is to find one of those peeps and make it work. But I don't know how to make it work—and that's the reason for this book!

Only women are allowed to change their mind.

Darlene

Darlene works at the should-be-world-famous Texas Hot Dogs in downtown Altoona, Pennsylvania. If you're ever in Altoona, you need to check it out and get a couple of dogs with sauce and some root beer. That's what's up! Senator Barack Obama stopped there when he was campaigning through Pennsylvania, and a few months later he became president. Coincidence . . . or Texas Hot Dogs?

Stefany 3/10/07

- Sometimes girls want meaning-less sex too... We don't always want want a relationship

- just tell the truth, it stops girls from getting psycho

- just because I'm walking around without a guy doesn't mean I want you to grab me.

- don't be afraid to court a girl, they like it sometimes

- We are hard to figure out, sorry about that, so really there is nothing you can do but figure us out an a personal level so good luck!

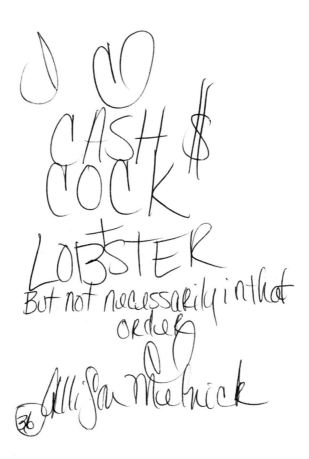

I ♡ CASH $
COCK
LOBSTER
But not necessarily in that order

Allison Melnick

Somebody *had* to say it!!!

Never say

no"

Shallow

we can't move

CHAPTER 10

MEN ARE DUMB

And women are gullible. Keep it movin'.

After reading these entries, I felt like guys should run for shelter 'cause we're under attack. But I guess men need to learn things the hard way sometimes. And trust me, if you are a man reading this chapter, a lot of this will be hard to swallow . . . thatswhatshesaid.

Just 'cuz I'm a redhead and a bartender and I'm nice to you in NO WAY means that I need your attention or would EVER talk to you in a non-tipping environment. I act like I don't like you because I DON'T LIKE you.

Kelly, bartender

You'll notice a recurring theme among the bartenders in the book. They're all a little . . . um . . . feisty. I have the feeling someone's tip cup is gonna be a little light after this book comes out.

Men need to understand that they're the crazy ones. We're here to keep them sane.

Mili

Women see things in a totally different perspective than men. It usually is a more sensitive, less harsh perspective.

Milan

"More sensitive, less harsh perspective"? Milan obviously doesn't watch *The View*. I mean, have you ever listened to a group of women sit around and talk about someone they don't like? Your first pull off of a Kool 100 is less harsh than that. Check out any episode of *The Real Housewives of [insert city here]* for proof.

Why do men have so much pride?! "It's better to lose your pride over someone you love than lose someone you love over pride."

Vida Guerra

Men don't know shit! Everything they know comes from women. Marriage is an endless education with the woman as the teacher.

Mea

Don't hold back, Mea. Tell us how you really feel. Oh, and by the way, I'll bet you have no idea what a hot route is . . . or a pick and roll . . . or a suicide squeeze . . . So therefore men *do* know sh*t!

Men should think twice before they speak because women mostly do, and that is why they take what you say to heart.

Adrienne

You are not cool when you scream out car windows when you see hot girls walking down the street. Girls hate it—it doesn't make us want to jump in your car and into your pants. Be respectful and don't approach girls like douchebags. They're much more likely to talk to you if you're just polite and respectful, so don't be a cocky asshole.

Christina

So yelling, "It must be jelly 'cause jam don't shake like that!" ain't gonna get me the digits? Damn, I've been going about this all wrong.

women are here to
smash men's ego.
plain & simple,
accept this truth
and life will be ea~~sier~~
better. [DEEP]

also women like it when
men tell them they look
nice. [shallow]

but both are true.
if you want more then ⟹

You will have to pay
for it.

So we got to Butter, and we're situated in a booth. Ashton gave me a proper introduction to her, since we were at different ends of the table at dinner earlier and didn't really have a chance to talk there. A few minutes later she leaned over and told me she wanted to check out the book. She'd seen someone else writing in it at dinner and was wondering what it was. I fished it out from my back pocket and handed it over. She took the book, and she and the friend she was sitting next to began to look through it. They laughed at some of the things that were written and seemed to be enjoying what they were reading. Then I saw her reach for her purse. I kind of paused for a second, wondering what she was up to. After she dug in her bag for a few seconds, she pulled out a pen. She then went to an empty page in the journal and began to write in it. Kutch turned to me and mouthed the words Holy Shit!, which was exactly what was going through my mind. Up until that point, the book was real to me, but I'm not sure how real it was to anyone else. I mean, there were a few more famous women in the history of the Earth—the Virgin Mary, Mother Teresa, Princess Di, and maybe Oprah—but getting Madonna, arguably the most famous female singer ever, involved, well, in those few seconds that it took for her to write an entry, shit got very real.

I don't ~~need~~ want men to know anything cause then I could no longer confuse them into submission

tinkerbell

25

smut peddler

Tinkerbell—and she assures me that is her name as it appears on her birth certificate—was working at the Hustler Store in West Hollywood and listed her occupation as "smut peddler." Makes the submission comment easier to understand.

Andrea ("The Czech chick")
24   waitress

Never say "no" to the woman
never disagree with her and
your life is gonna be great.
Remember: Man maybe the
"head" in the relationship
but woman is the "neck".
And u can't move your head
without the neck!
        Love Andrea

continue in Czech

→

Nikdy nepovedz "nie" žene.
Vždy s ňou súhlas a tvoj
život bude úžasný!!!
pamätaj: Muž je "možno"
"hlavou" vo vzťahu ale
žena je "hrdlo". A bez krku
hlavou nepohneš!

S láskou
Andrea

Guess what . . . Unfortunately, it's not what men need to understand about women . . . it's really what women need to understand about men . . . MEN ARE CAPABLE OF BEING EMOTIONALLY UNATTACHED. They could be in love and blissfully happy with their woman but still be able to FUCK another woman (skank)—without it affecting his feelings for his lady! It's up to the woman whether she's strong enough to stand by her man or move on. THAT'S THE TRUTH . . . At least as far as the whole land of LALA [Los Angeles] is concerned!

Darling Nikki

I agree that most men probably could be with another woman without changing his feelings for his lady. It's just up to him to restrict and not give in to temptation when involved in a committed relationship—and I'm pretty sure that applies everywhere, not just L.A.

Being a woman isn't as easy as it looks. There are two challenges we must face every day.

1. Fighting the aging process and praying we don't wake up one morning looking like our favorite designer handbag.

2. Fighting being crazy.

I'll give an example of the latter. Sometimes there are things with men that you just have to give a little slack. One being the ability to keep their attention during a conversation. Generally, a man's ability to pay attention to a cackling woman has all the stability of an Etch A Sketch. To keep his attention, you need to realize that generally he's not going to want to hear the Bible. He's going to want the Cliffs Notes instead. Before a guy tunes us out and puts us in the category of Charlie Brown's teacher, where "wah wah wah" is all he hears, we should treat the conversation as if we're giving a presentation at work. Summarize and hit those bullet points to keep his attention. The ease of a man tuning out happens for the same reason a dog licks his balls . . . because HE CAN.

Marisa Tellez, age thirty-four,
production coordinator for television

This one seems to be directed more at women than men, which is fine . . . 'cause all I can think about is if we could be like that dog, all of this discussion would be unnecessary!!!

I sometimes wish that men could be in a woman's body for two days (a week would be a dream). Then they would understand us and why our minds think the way they do. When did they forget that we don't think like them???
Men are definitely from Mars. If they could experience life on Venus for one day I think the world would be an easier place to have a relationship and communicate.

Stacy Keibler

Stacy, I also wish that a man could be in a woman's body for a week . . . but probably for FAR different reasons than you're talking about!!!

What men should know about women:

- They never want just 25 percent of your time, they want 100 percent of your time, no matter what they say.

- Always make the lady you are with feel like she is the most beautiful girl in the room.

- If you smoke and she hates it, then pretend like you don't.

- Every girl loves Snoop Dog!!

- Never have sex to Lionel Richie, only have sex to Marvin Gaye!!!

- Learn that "yo bitch" is not going to get you any ass!

- Guys wearing matching hats and shirts are lame!!! Even if you are from Brooklyn!!!

- Honesty is the best trait any man can have.

Brittanie

Somewhere in this book I wrote about girls being complex . . . 'Nuff said!

you don't like me.

in the history of
man/woman kind.

well

not me. :")

CHAPTER 11

BE A MAN

Women are always saying, *"Be a man."* Well, this next chapter will tell you what women think constitutes true "manly behavior." These aren't things that should offend a guy. Unless he's not handling his business correctly.

I wish guys would stop being so girly. I wish guys would step up and be like a male and take care of a flat tire or any other male duty in need. Be a man and not a Hollywood whore.

Sarah

Or if you live in Sheboygan, don't be a Sheboygan whore!

Strong, powerful, and confident men have always been a major part in my life. My father was a prison guard and also the King of the Castle when I was little. Now I work in a very male dominated industry—professional wrestling. All these powerful men and boys have taught me sooo many priceless lessons. The biggest lesson that no matter how strong I think I am and no matter how many wrestling matches I have had I am still just a girl. These amazing men not only take care of us girls while driving from town to town, but also while partying around the world. These men are our protectors. What

I wish all men understood about women is even if our jobs are wrestlers or teachers, designers, doctors or stay at home mothers—make sure to treat us like ladies. We women are still figuring out the balance between family, men, friends, jobs and things we love. So men should understand sometimes we just need someone to lean on. Don't call us crazy (even when we are) if you don't understand. Trust me, calling anyone crazy makes them crazy. Just ask us to explain. Just listen. By the time we are done crying and talking we already feel better. We don't need to be completely understood. We just want to be accepted in all of our womanly glory . . . with ALL of our flaws. Protect us, nurture the little girl within and respect the women we are.

Maria Kanellis, WWE Diva

If you are a man in Maria's life, you would do yourself a great favor by making sure you treat her right. The last thing in the world you would want is a knock on your door from Mr. K the prison guard . . . or, God forbid, the Undertaker and the Big Show coming by to pay you a visit.

Jac Vanek - 20 - LA

I have this Theory
that boys who love
cats are the same
type of boys who ~~is~~ are
afraid of roller coasters.
IF you fall into this
category, don't talk
to me. I don't know
how other women view
this issue, but personally

It is the biggest turn-
off in the history of
man/woman kind. Maybe
the cavewomen didn't
agree, but fuck them.
PS- open a friggin door
one of these days.
You could definitely get
a girl into bed just by
that (well not me. :))
Be nice boys
jac Vanek

Don't be a mama's boy. Don't come off too strong and don't ever tell a woman to run away with you on your first date. And ALWAYS respect and compliment them.

Anna

Les hommes doivent comprendre qu'ils ne se marieont pas avec leurs potes! Et donc depenser leur energy dans leur relation plutot que dans les sorties entre amis!

Un homme attirant, est un grand homme/homme adult pas un—petit garçon!

Floriane

TRANSLATION:
Men have to understand that they are not going to marry their buddies! So they should spend their energy on their relationships, not in going out with their friends!

An attractive man is a grown man—not a little boy!

Hmm . . . So many things. First of all, men need to stop taking on the emotional-girl role and BE A MAN!!! I mean, I'm an L.A. native, born and raised, and 99 percent of guys I've dated have had absolutely no clue as to how to take on the male role. Most men I've come across are more of a girl than I am. That's sad.

Secondly, I wish guys could just grasp a better general understanding of the female race. We're not really as complex as you seem to think . . .

Here's three vital things to keep a woman happy (every man should memorize these three things):

1.   When we argue with you, at least ACT like you hear us, okay?!?

2.   Good sex. You're not the only one here that would like a goddamn orgasm from time to time . . . and stop being lazy!

3.   Always keep in mind that if all else fails, a little blue Tiffany's box is always a great problem solver.

Blake

HOTTEST

mans body

Pick up the phone
and send
the flowers

Surprising

CHAPTER 12

THE LITTLE THINGS

These are the things, men, that can put you over the top in a relationship. It seems like most women appreciate and enjoy the little, heartfelt expressions more than anything else. Pay attention and reap the benefits!

Surprising a girl w/ flowers, dinner, or anything that she didn·t ask you to do will get you A LOT . . .

Lenkn

I'm not sure if I agree with this one because *all* guys have tried surprising a girl with a few things and . . . *welllllll*, let's just say it doesn't always pan out, *youknowwhatumsayin?* But this does seem like solid, foolproof advice.

Men need to understand that real women don't need money to be happy.

Marina

Then can you explain why the fifty-five-year-old billionaire ends up with the twenty-year-old supermodel? Guess it has more to do with his charming personality than his private jet, right?!?

It is amazing how the smallest gesture can show a woman how much a man cares. Most women I know would prefer their partner to light a single candle during a stay-at-home dinner as opposed to having his assistant call and reserve the best table at the most expensive restaurant. It's almost amazing how little effort is required to please us. A simple compliment can often leave a smile on our faces for the rest of the day. We just need to know we are not taken for granted and that chivalry and romance can still exist long after a relationship has moved into the comfort phase. Your attention is what we crave. Kindness and honesty is key—better to be told the truth than be in a relationship full of deceit (well, most of the time!). Be truthful, dammit!! Women are fantastic, beautiful, complex beings. We ARE a bit nutty, so be patient with us and we won't let you down.

Jenny

It's great that Jenny likes small gestures, because that's all that most guys are able to muster. It's good to know that we don't always have to hire a marching band or have a plane skywrite "I Love You." Give them smooches (girls looove smooches) and generally be nice to them—that seems to be key.

guys. if you want to get
our clothes off
focus on what you're giving
not on what you can get!

You may be able to score, once-
but we can smell the stink
of selfish desire a mile away
and are not interested.

Women are caretakers by nature
don't take it for granted.
The romance we are looking for comes
from feeling appreciated-
Notice the little things
And you'll get everything!

demi Moore
"Mrs Kutcher"

Demi and I used to be roommates. Yes, you read it right. For roughly two and a half years, Demi and her three daughters, Ashton, and I all lived together—kind of like a new style Brady Bunch. I have had the pleasure of sharing many great times with her. Thank you for helping to validate this book . . . and for not making your future hubby kick me out of the house when you moved in! Molly, you in danger girl!

All girls want to feel special,
and it's really easy to make
them feel that way. Pick
up the phone and send the
girl you love flowers.
Put in a little effort and
we'll be putty in your
hands.

♡ Sheroum Kim
    23 years old
    Director's Asst.
    9/8/07

My first, most important thing to say is "BE YOURSELF!!" Open up and love yourself before you can, or THINK you can, commit to a woman. Women just want you to LOVE them and pay attention to them. You don't have to buy them things or take them out to fancy dinners. Just show them that you want to be with them ... pizza, movie, museum, whatever ... but pull through and don't be scared to commit! "MEN" make my world go around!

Yael

- Men should know that women appreciate simple things and surprises—a card to say "I was thinking about your lips," or a surprise visit just because being around her makes him happy.

- Men should also know that they are amazing friends to women and I love them for this (and so much more). To all the men who make women smile and kiss their girlfriends or wives with passion (even after the years)—I thank you! Until we meet again, always ...

Katia

I believe gifts are in the uncertainty. Men shouldn't know everything. They should find what is in their hearts and don't hold back. Don't be afraid. Show who you are from the start, and if the woman reciprocates, move forward, and if not, move on and find the right one. Most of all, laugh. If you can't be silly with the woman ... move on.

Nicole

From a woman who has known a lot of men . . . I don't know if there is a common language. It's yin and yang and the true beauty is in the opposites. There may be "understanding," and maybe not, but there is definitely a journey into the unknown. And the adventure in all its ups and downs is what we are all after. Love me, hurt me, use me, appreciate me, see me, ignore me . . . it's all part of it. There is no understanding. There is constant creation of something new. Life is born every day.

Melanie

A lot of men . . . Now, when you say a lot, are we talking about enough to field the starting lineup for the Mets, or a number that Leonidas would feel comfortable going into battle against the Persians with?

Okay, brother, let me start off by saying . . . study who you are interested in . . . Will she make you happy? And if not, how much do you need her? And your answer will determine if she's worth what you are achieving . . . Don't give her what you cannot receive before you start this process . . . know it . . .

DJ Bianca G

You always have to trust your heart. Seriously, if you don't learn from your own mistakes you will never know what others are up to. ALWAYS TRUST YOUR HEART!!! And you know what? If it doesn't work out, there's always more to come . . . and more than likely it'll be BETTER! Just always TRUST YOUR INSTINCT!! Trust me!

Brooke

But our instincts are telling us not to trust you . . . so where does that leave us?

What I'd like men to know . . .

You can never say too many sweet things . . . as long as it is authentic, we'll feel it and be grateful. A foot rub or a hot bath with candles—DIVINE—any day. Our beauty and grace shine when we are empowered—never fear or try to sabotage our empowerment—we often do a good job of that ourselves :) . . .

There is nothing more sexy than a man taking care of, spending time with, bonding with children . . .

Listen a lot . . . Keep your heart open . . . Tell the truth—we can handle it—even when it sucks . . .

Chocolate makes me happy. ☺

Andrea

OK. I got a lot to say on the matter. But first, Chivalry is the new black. Never underestimate the power of THOUGHTFULNESS. Remember the small stuff. Details. You will earn major points. And frankly, It's just cool. (example: Remember her favorite flower / favorite car / football team) That said — when courting: LESS IS MORE. Don't expose all your cards before the game starts (This applies to texting, emailing, IM ing, Whatever) Just chill. Maintain the mystery in the courtship phase. THAT SAID — — Be decisive - assertin. Not to be confused with PUSHY. PUSHY sucks ass. Ugly.

P.S.
YOU GUYS
DO KNOW WHAT
TO DO -- Its up to you
if you want to actually
do it.

And LAST but definatdy

NOT least : The HOTTEST

Part of a mans body is

His BIG FAT SWEATY

SEXY SENSE OF HUMOR.

HOPE THIS HELPS

FEB 12 2008
The Standard
Hotel - L.A.

XOXO

Lake

Lake Bell

Girls like the little things. Keep it simple...they matter the most. A compliment goes a long way.

Christina

I guess that depends on how she takes the compliment. I told a girl that she was thicker than a bowl of oatmeal, which I meant as a nod to her sexiness. She sucked her teeth and rolled her eyes at me and kept it moving. Clearly my compliment did not go a long way.

Men need to know when women are in a bad mood or when they need something __without__ us women having to tell them. They just need to __know__ without having to be asked for. It might not make any sense for men but Im sure women will know what I mean.

Angelika

Men and women are different in this main and important way: If you think of brains as roads, a man's brain is a windy, dusty country road. A woman's brain is a superhighway—twelve lanes, rush-hour traffic 24/7. It's not a choice, it's a birthright. Men, as much as you need to understand this metaphor, it's also helpful to point it out to women when they say things like "What are you thinking?" The answer is oftentimes "nothing." That's pretty hard for women to understand, as our brains are firing five hundred thoughts at one time. So if your girl thinks you're hiding things from her, just say, "Baby, my mind is like a quiet country road." The best way to deal with this difference is to just LET YOUR WOMAN SPEAK. It doesn't matter if you think all of her issues and complaints are petty, uninteresting, and boring—do NOT let her know that you think this! Make her feel heard, make her feel important, make her feel loved! We don't need you to fix our problems, we just want you to listen to them! Also . . . women usually want sex as much as you do, but if we initiate it we feel like a ho, so come and get it! If you live with a woman you damn well better take the trash out once a day and empty the litter box once a week on your own . . . WITHOUT HER HAVING TO ASK. Women don't care about your burping and farting. We do care when you can't get it up. Sorry, but true. Open doors, pull out chairs, bring flowers, write notes. It's the thought that matters, not the money.

Karyn

To understand a woman:

Well, I can't really speak for all women, but I can speak from experiences I've had and what 99 percent of my girlfriends constantly complain about and search for. So here it goes: There is still such a thing as chivalry. It's really the little things that add up to big things that we learn to appreciate, know, and love. Open a door, walk her to her doorstep! Take her on a date before you try to hook up with her. If she's worth it, a girl with quality, you can wait a little. You may think you listen, but the truth is, you probably don't. Remember the important things: birthdays, special dates, etc. Most importantly, for me anyway—laugh, have fun, be yourself. It's true, we don't always want to cuddle, drop everything we're doing to cater to you, and in the morning, we're not always "in the mood." But if you're worth it—well, just be worth it.

Tristen

Living in L.A. for the last few years, I have learned that it's much harder to find that person who makes us want to go the extra mile (for a whole list of reasons that we'll save for another day), but I agree if you find one who's worth it, it's a beautiful thing.

only in movies.

one of
millions...

you?

First I would like to start by saying,
ALL members of the female population
expect different things.

CHAPTER 13

THE PERFECT MAN

The thing about "The Perfect Man"—he doesn't exist. He can't exist. Why, you ask? Because women are a fickle bunch. If you've read this book and have reached this point, then you'll clearly see that they can't agree on whether or not we should lie to them or tell them the truth. So there's no chance of them agreeing to the perfect components that would create a consummate male. One girl did try, though—she gave me the recipe to her ideal man pie:

"Look like Marlon Brando. [I take it she means Brando from *The Wild One*, not *The Freshman*.] Listen like Philip Seymour Hoffman. [Clearly noted for his auditory skills.] Sing like Jeff Buckley. ["Grace" . . . I get it.] Charm like Valmont.

[Malkovich or Philippe?] Dance like Michael. [Long Live the King!] Think like Obama.

[Say no more.]"

See the conundrum? Pretty impossible to meet that criteria.

My friend Krista was also up to the challenge. It's almost as if she had stockpiled these thoughts. Although she stopped short of a dissertation, she clearly had loads of suggestions, in case the subject was ever brought up. Which it was. So enjoy the lessons being shared. And try to keep up.

My first thought is, "Well, if men can't figure that out on their own, then that is their problem!"

But it just hit me. Based on that selfish theory, it seems the answer to your burning question is crystal clear . . . We just want men to read our minds! I mean, if you really want to be with us you should just KNOW what we expect from you without us having to risk looking like the needy creatures we are and having to tell you, dammit! That said, there are a few words of "wisdom" to keep in your playbook.

Men need to know that women want to be cherished. We want you to send us cute text messages out of the blue telling us that you miss us! Even if we've only been apart a few hours . . . JUST DO IT! Also, you get huge bonus points for the occasional wall posting on Facebook that sounds sexy and mysterious and like something only your girl will understand. We love this stuff because when our girlfriends ask what it means (and they will) we get to brag about how adorable you were the other night when, after our third hour of rolling around in bed, we fell asleep with smiles on our faces and you held me all night. It puts us in the Queen Bee category with our friends and it makes us feel special. And for the record, if the relationship doesn't work out, your ex will have a hard time convincing all her friends that you're a TOTAL loser-jerk. Side note: This kind of doting only applies if you know for a FACT that the feeling is mutual and she really likes you. Just make the extra effort to let her know you are thinking about her and always remind her that she is beautiful and has a sexy body. Flattery might not get you everywhere, but it will get you most places.

However, if you have a mad crush on someone who doesn't reciprocate... PLEASE don't do the stalking, calling, desperate-man thing like sending random pizzas to her house with pepperoni-laden messages that read "YOU COMPLETE ME"... Because it's LAME and so not cute when it's coming from the wrong guy. When stuff like that happens, we get annoyed and we pity you. Not to mention you're sure to be the punch line of many jokes at the next girls' night dinner. The only exception to that rule is if you think she's playing hard to get. But you must have solid evidence to back that theory up. Go with your gut on that one, but please be honest with yourself.

Sometimes we need a little aloofness to pique our interest and secure you a place in our hearts. In this case, "Ignore me and I'm yours" is our secret mantra, and we are just testing you. Women like the chase; we want to know you want us and we want you to prove it... but we can't know for sure we really want you if you never let us miss you. And if you ignore her after your initial attempt at trying to get her attention and she still doesn't come around, then she is simply not interested. At this point, step away from the hottie.

Women love confidence, success, security, and power in a man. We want to know that he can take care of us, or at the very least has the potential to do so. There is no bigger turnoff than a guy who still lives at home with his mother, who has no real job and isn't sure what he wants to do with his life. He can have the greatest ideas about things he wants to do, but if there is no follow-through, the woman will have no respect and inevitably walk away.

Some guys think that they can make up for their lack of ambition and follow-through if they simply absorb themselves into their woman's life and make her into their "job." Please don't do this, guys. Have your own social life. The scenario above always ends in tears for the slacker dude (not to mention he will forever be branded with a creepy and controlling reputation) because all that "unconditional" support and "well-meaning" co-dependent advice you give her will be taken into another relationship with the guy she left you for that actually has his shit together.

And you will be left a bitter shell of a man who turns to antidepressants to fill the void.

Oh . . . and please take showers every day so you don't smell like a homeless person. B.O. is really not sexy. And no woman wants to be with a guy who wears the same boxers for five days.

Krista Allen

OUTRO

Well, it was a quite a trip to get to this point. Six years after first getting my mitts on *Everything Men Understand About Women,* we end this part of the journey here. What have I really learned? Well, men and women are almost identical in what we want and need from each other as partners. The route taken to get to each destination is very different, but the end destination is the same. I've realized that life would be less fun if men and women were always on the same page. Figuring out what makes each other tick is a huge part of the relationship process and I guess of life in general. Embrace the things that make each other different and unique. And may I remind you of this most true piece of wisdom from Jessica:

Stop trying to understand bitches. We're all different. Learn how to handle YOUR bitch and leave it at that.

I couldn't have said it better myself!

ACKNOWLEDGMENTS

To Thea and Tamika—you two had the best experience ever: the pleasure of having me as a big brother! Could ya ask for anything more? For having to put up with me—I thank you. ❋ To all my family members who now number well into the thousands—for the teachings, knowledge, and fun—I thank you. ❋ To Grandma Easter for teaching me to love the Lord and sweet potato pie and to Grandpa James for teaching me to love a well-told story and pro wrestling—I thank you. ❋ To Mike "Animal" Theroux for that ride from Pittsburgh to L.A. back in '99— I thank you. ❋ To Matty—we share pretty much the same stories. For being a great friend—I thank you. ❋ To Big Wil—for years of great friendship and ridiculous generosity. And for keeping my rent more than reasonably affordable—I thank you. ❋ To Ashton—for being able to take anyone at all on your ride with you, and for whatever reason allowing me to ride shotgun. And for genuinely being one of the best friends I have ever had—I thank you! ❋ To Becka Oliver, my agent at WME—for taking an interest in me and my idea and helping me get to . . . here.—I thank you. ❋ To Suzanne and Carrie—for your deft skills as editors and for deciphering my less-than-by-the-book writing style—I thank you. ❋ To the friends I've made in Altoona, Pittsburgh, and L.A.—for helping me grow and evolve—I thank you. ❋ To the women who took part in this project—clearly without ALL of you, this wouldn't be possible—I thank you. ❋ Last but not least, to my mom, Linda. Remember when I'd run around the kitchen telling you I wanted to be Superman or the Hulk or a Dallas Cowboy? You never discouraged me. And although I never did land a career as the Hulk, hopefully you aren't too disappointed. I always wanted to do something to make you proud—hopefully this is it. *Now* you can brag—I love you!